Jonathan Barnes

ARISTOTLE

A Very Short Introduction

OXFORD
UNIVERSITY PRESS

OXFORD
UNIVERSITY PRESS

Great Clarendon Street, Oxford OX2 6DP

Oxford University Press is a department of the University of Oxford.
It furthers the University's objective of excellence in research, scholarship,
and education by publishing worldwide in

Oxford New York

Athens Auckland Bangkok Bogotá Buenos Aires Calcutta
Cape Town Chennai Dar es Salaam Delhi Florence Hong Kong Istanbul
Karachi Kuala Lumpur Madrid Melbourne Mexico City Mumbai
Nairobi Paris São Paulo Shanghai Singapore Taipei Tokyo Toronto Warsaw

with associated companies in Berlin Ibadan

Oxford is a registered trade mark of Oxford University Press
in the UK and in certain other countries

Published in the United States
by Oxford University Press Inc., New York

© Jonathan Barnes 2000

British Library Cataloguing in Publication Data
Data available

Library of Congress Cataloging in Publication Data
Data available

ISBN 0-19-285408-9

1 3 5 7 9 10 8 6 4 2

Typeset by RefineCatch Ltd, Bungay, Suffolk
Printed in Spain by Book Print S. L.

Contents

For Richard Robinson

List of Illustrations

The publisher and the author apologize for any errors or omissions in the above list. If contacted they will be pleased to rectify these at the earliest opportunity.

List of Maps

Chapter 1
The Man and His Work

Aristotle died in the autumn of 322 BC. He was sixty-two and at the height of his powers: a scholar whose scientific explorations were as wide-ranging as his philosophical speculations were profound; a teacher who enchanted and inspired the brightest youth of Greece; a public figure who lived a turbulent life in a turbulent world. He bestrode antiquity like an intellectual colossus. No man before him had contributed so much to learning. No man after him might aspire to rival his achievements.

Of Aristotle's character and personality little is known. He came from a rich family. He was allegedly a dandy, wearing rings on his fingers and cutting his hair fashionably short. He suffered from poor digestion, and is said to have been spindle-shanked. He was a good speaker, lucid in his lectures, persuasive in conversation; and he had a mordant wit. His enemies, who were numerous, accused him of arrogance. His will, which has survived, is a generous document. His philosophical writings are impersonal; but they suggest that he prized both friendship and self-sufficiency, and that, while conscious of his place in an honourable tradition, he was properly proud of his own attainments. As a man, he was, perhaps, admirable rather than amiable.

That is thin material for a biographer; and we may not hope to know Aristotle as we might know Albert Einstein or Bertrand Russell – he

1. 'Aristotle was a dandy, wearing rings on his fingers and cutting his hair fashionably short.' The sculptor of this bust – perhaps a copy of one commissioned by Alexander the Great – saw him otherwise.

lived too long ago and the abyss of time has swallowed up the facts of his life. One thing, however, can be said with reasonable confidence: throughout his life Aristotle was driven by one overmastering desire – the desire for knowledge. His whole career and his every known activity testify to the fact: he was concerned before all else to promote the discovery of truth and to increase the sum of human knowledge.

He did not think himself singular in possessing such a desire, even if he pursued his object with a singular devotion; for he affirmed that 'all men by nature desire to know', and he claimed that each one of us is, most properly speaking, to be identified with his mind, so that life – a fully human life – is 'the activity of the mind'. In an early work, the *Protrepticus* or *Exhortation to Philosophy*, Aristotle announced that 'the acquisition of wisdom is pleasant; all men feel at home in philosophy and wish to spend time on it, leaving all other things aside'. The word 'philosophy' designates, etymologically, the love of wisdom; and a philosopher, in Aristotle's book, is not a cloistered academic engaged in remote and abstract speculation – he is someone who searches for 'knowledge of things human and divine'. In one of his later works, the *Nicomachean Ethics*, Aristotle argues that 'happiness' – that state of mind in which men realize themselves and flourish best – consists in a life of intellectual activity. Is not such a life too godlike for mere mortals to sustain? No; for 'we must not listen to those who urge us to think human thoughts since we are human, and mortal thoughts since we are mortal; rather, we should as far as possible immortalize ourselves and do all we can to live by the finest element in us – for if in bulk it is small, in power and worth it is far greater than anything else'.

A man's proper aim is to immortalize himself, to imitate the gods; for in doing so he becomes most fully a man and most fully himself. Such self-realization requires him to act on that desire for knowledge which as a man he naturally possesses. Aristotle's recipe for 'happiness' may be thought severe or restricted, and he was surely optimistic in ascribing to the generality of mankind his own passionate desire for learning. But his recipe came from the heart: he counsels us to live our lives as he himself tried to live his own.

One of Aristotle's ancient biographers remarks that 'he wrote a large number of books which I have thought it appropriate to list because of the man's excellence in every field': there follows a list of some 150 items, which, taken together and published in the modern style, would amount to perhaps fifty substantial volumes of print. And the list does not include all of Aristotle's writings – indeed, it fails to mention two of the works, the *Metaphysics* and the *Nicomachean Ethics*, for which he is today most renowned. It is a vast output; yet it is more remarkable for its scope and variety than for its quantity. The catalogue of his titles includes *On Justice, On the Poets, On Wealth, On the Soul, On Pleasure, On the Sciences, On Species and Genus, Deductions, Definitions, Lectures on Political Theory* (in eight books), *The Art of Rhetoric, On the Pythagoreans, On Animals* (in nine books), *Dissections* (in seven books), *On Plants, On Motion, On Astronomy, Homeric Problems* (in six books), *On Magnets, Olympic Victors, Proverbs, On the River Nile*. There are works on logic and on language; on the arts; on ethics and politics and law; on constitutional history and on intellectual history; on psychology and physiology; on natural history – zoology, biology, botany; on chemistry, astronomy, mechanics, mathematics; on the philosophy of science and on the nature of motion and space and time; on metaphysics and the theory of knowledge. Choose a field of research, and Aristotle laboured in it; pick an area of human endeavour, and Aristotle discoursed upon it.

Of all these writings barely one-fifth has survived. But the surviving fraction contains samples of most of his studies, and although the major part of his life's work is lost, we may still form a rounded idea of his activities.

Most of the surviving writings were perhaps never intended to be read;

for it seems likely that the treatises which we possess were made up from Aristotle's lecture notes. The notes were made for his own use and not for public dissemination. They were no doubt tinkered with over a period of years. Moreover, although some of the treatises owe their structure to Aristotle himself, others were plainly put together by later editors – the *Nicomachean Ethics* is evidently not a unitary work, the *Metaphysics* is plainly a set of essays rather than a continuous treatise. In the light of this, it will hardly be a surprise to find that the style of Aristotle's works is often rugged. Plato's dialogues are finished literary artefacts, the subtleties of their thought matched by the tricks of their language. Aristotle's writings for the most part are terse. His arguments are concise. There are abrupt transitions, inelegant repetitions, obscure allusions. Paragraphs of continuous exposition are set among staccato jottings. The language is spare and sinewy. If the treatises are unpolished, that is in part because Aristotle had felt no need and no urge to take down the beeswax. But only in part; for Aristotle had reflected on the appropriate style for scientific writing and he favoured simplicity. 'In every form of instruction there is some small need to pay attention to language; for it makes a difference with regard to making things clear whether we speak in this or that way. But it does not make *much* of a difference: all these things are show and directed at the hearer – which is why no one teaches geometry in this way.' Aristotle could write finely – his style was praised by ancient critics who read works of his which we cannot – and some parts of the surviving items are done with power and even with panache. But fine words butter no parsnips, and fine language yields no scientific profit.

The reader who opens his Aristotle and expects to find a systematic disquisition on some philosophical subject or an orderly textbook of scientific instruction, will be brought up short: Aristotle's treatises are not like that. But reading the treatises is not a dull slog. Aristotle has a vigour which is the more attractive the better it is known; and the treatises, which have none of the camouflage of Plato's dialogues, reveal their author's thoughts – or at least appear to do so – in a direct and stark fashion. It is easy to imagine that you can overhear Aristotle talking to himself.

Above all, Aristotle is tough. A good way of reading him is this: Take up a treatise, think of it as a set of lecture notes, and imagine that you now have to lecture from them. You must expand and illustrate the argument, and you must make the transitions clear; you will probably decide to relegate certain paragraphs to footnotes, or reserve them for another time and another lecture; and if you have any talent at all as a lecturer, you will find that the jokes add themselves. Let it be admitted that Aristotle can be not only tough but also vexing. Whatever does he mean here? How on earth is this conclusion supposed to follow from those premises? Why this sudden barrage of technical terms? One ancient critic claimed that 'he surrounds the difficulty of his subject with the obscurity of his language, and thus avoids refutation – producing darkness, like a squid, in order to make himself hard to capture'. Every reader will, from time to time, think of Aristotle as a squid. But the moments of vexation are outnumbered by the moments of elation. Aristotle's treatises offer a peculiar challenge to their readers; and once you have taken up the challenge, you would not have the treatises in any other form.

Chapter 2
A Public Figure

Aristotle was no recluse: the life of contemplation which he commends is not to be spent in an armchair or an ivory tower. He was never a politician, but he was a public figure and lived often enough in the public gaze. Yet in the spring of 322 he retired to Chalcis on the island of Euboea, where his mother's family had property; and in the last months of his life he lamented his isolation.

The preceding thirteen years he had spent in Athens, the cultural capital of the Greek world. There he had taught regularly, in the Lyceum. For he believed that knowledge and teaching were inseparable. His own researches were frequently carried out in company, in a research team; and he communicated his results to his friends and pupils, never thinking of them as a private treasure-store – after all, a man cannot claim to know a subject unless he is capable of transmitting his knowledge to others, and teaching is the best proof and the natural manifestation of knowledge.

The Lyceum is sometimes referred to as Aristotle's 'school'; and it is tempting to think of it as a sort of modern university: timetables and lecture courses and a syllabus, the enrolment of students and their examination, and the granting of degrees. But the Lyceum was not a private college: it was a public place – a sanctuary and a gymnasium. An old story tells that Aristotle lectured to his chosen pupils in the

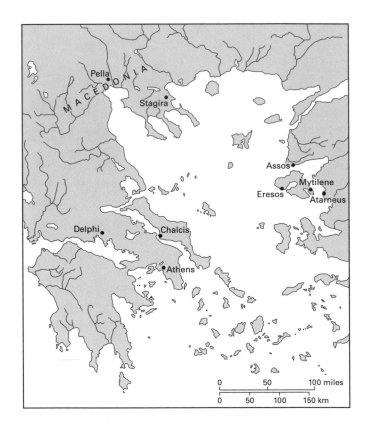

Map 1. Map of Greece indicating Aristotle's places of work.

mornings and to the general public in the evenings. However that may be, arrangements in the Lyceum were surely less formal than those of a university. There were no examinations and no degrees; there were no student fees (and no student grants); there was none of that Byzantine bureaucracy without which no modern professor can teach and no modern student learn.

Aristotle combined teaching and research – his lectures must often have been 'research papers', or talks based on his current research interests. He did not work alone. Various colleagues joined him in his scientific and philosophical enterprises. In truth, we know little enough about all this: for myself, I like to think of a group of friends working in concert, rather than of a Teutonic professor directing the projects of his abler students; but that is fancy.

Why did Aristotle suddenly abandon the pleasures of the Lyceum and retire to Chalcis? He allegedly said that 'he did not want the Athenians to commit a second crime against philosophy'. The first crime had been Socrates' trial and execution. Aristotle feared that he might suffer Socrates' fate, and his fears had a political basis.

During Aristotle's lifetime, Macedonia, under the rule first of Philip II and then of his son, Alexander the Great, expanded its power and came to dominate the Greek world, depriving the small city-states of their independence and of some of their liberties. Aristotle had lifelong connections with Macedonia: before his birth, his father, Nicomachus, had been a physician at the Macedonian court; and at his death his will named Antipater, Alexander's viceroy in Greece, as his executor. The most famous episode in the Macedonian story began in 343: Philip invited Aristotle to Mieza as tutor to the young Alexander, and Aristotle stayed at court for a couple of years or so. A rich romance came to surround that happy coupling of prince and philosopher; and we shall not hope to see through the fog of legend or determine how far Aristotle influenced his ambitious and unlovely charge. No doubt he

2. 'Philip invited Aristotle to Mieza as tutor to the young Alexander, and Aristotle stayed at court for a couple of years or so. A rich romance came to surround that happy coupling of prince and philosopher.' Medieval manuscripts sometimes illustrated the romance.

profited from his royal position; and perhaps he also used his influence for the good of others – we are told (and the story may, for all I know, be true) that the Athenians set up an inscription in his honour, recording that he 'had served the city well . . . by all his services to the people of Athens, especially by intervening with King Philip for the purpose of promoting their interests'.

Alexander died in June of 323. Many Athenians were pleased by the news, and anti-Macedonian feelings were not disguised. Aristotle was not a Macedonian agent. (And it is worth remarking that the political philosophy which he taught in the Lyceum contained no apology for Macedonian imperialism: on the contrary, it was against empire and against emperors.) None the less, Aristotle was associated with Macedonia. He had had a Macedonian past, and he still had Macedonian friends. He found it prudent to leave Athens.

A sidelight is shed by a broken inscription which archaeologists discovered some seventy years ago at Delphi. The fragment records that since 'they drew up a table of those who won victories in both Pythian Games and of those who from the beginning organized the contest, let Aristotle and Callisthenes be praised and crowned; and let the Stewards transcribe the table . . . and set it up in the temple'. The inscription was engraved in about 330 BC. Some years later, Aristotle allegedly wrote to his friend Antipater in the following vein: 'as for what was voted to me at Delphi, of which I am now deprived, this is my attitude: I am neither greatly concerned by the matter, nor wholly unconcerned'. It seems that the honours voted to Aristotle in 330 were later withdrawn. The inscription was smashed, and it was discovered at the bottom of a well – did the jubilant democrats of Delphi hurl it there in 323 BC in a fit of anti-Macedonian pique?

However that may be, the fact that Aristotle was invited to draw up the victory lists at Delphi is evidence that by the 330s he had some reputation as a man of science. For the work demanded historical research. Victors in the Pythian Games, which were second in importance only to the Olympics, had their names and achievements preserved in the Delphic archives. Aristotle and Callisthenes (who was his nephew) must have sifted through a mass of ancient documents; from that material they had to determine a correct chronology, and then produce an authoritative list. The list was part of the history of sport; but it was also more than that. In Aristotle's day historians could not order their narratives by reference to a generally accepted system of chronological conventions (as modern historians use the conventions of BC and AD). Chronology, and hence accurate history, depended on synchronisms: 'The war broke out when X was chief magistrate at Athens, in the third year of the nth Olympiad, when Y won the chariot race at Delphi'. It was not until centuries after Aristotle's death that the problems of historical chronology were settled; but Aristotle had made some small contribution to the subject.

The list of Aristotle's writings to which I have already referred duly contains the title *Pythian Victors*. Alongside it are other titles testifying to similar projects of historical scholarship: *Olympic Victors*, *Didaskaliae* (a *catalogue raisonné* of the plays produced at the Athenian dramatic festivals), *Dikaiomata* (a collection of legal submissions made by various Greek cities which Aristotle prepared in order that Philip might settle boundary disputes). But of all such historical researches, the most remarkable are the *Constitutions of States*. There were 158 of them in all. A few fragments survive, quoted by later authors; and then, just over a century ago, the sands of Egypt delivered up a papyrus roll which contained almost the whole text of the *Constitution of the Athenians*. The work is in two parts: the first contains a brief constitutional history of Athens, the second offers a descriptive survey of Athenian political institutions in the fourth century BC. Aristotle, who was not himself a citizen of Athens, had presumably burrowed in the Athenian archives; he had read up the Athenian historians; and he had familiarized himself with Athenian political practices. His researches produced a compact and well-documented history of one aspect of Athenian life.

Chapter 3
Zoological Researches

Aristotle began teaching in the Lyceum in 335 BC. The thirteen years from 335 to 322 were his second Athenian period. His first period in Athens had lasted for twenty years, from 367 to 347. In 347 he suddenly left the city. No reason for his removal is reliably reported; but in 348 the northern town of Olynthus had fallen to the Macedonian army, and a hostile reaction had brought Demosthenes and his anti-Macedonian allies to power in Athens: it is likely enough that political issues drove Aristotle from Athens in 347 as they would drive him from Athens in 322.

For whatever reason, he sailed east across the Aegean and settled at Atarneus, a town with which he had family ties; and the 'tyrant' or ruler of Atarneus, Hermias by name, was a friend both of philosophy and of Macedonia. Hermias gave Aristotle and his companions 'the city of Assos to live in; and they spent their time there in philosophy, meeting together in a courtyard, and Hermias provided them with all they needed'.

Aristotle stayed in Assos for two or three years. He then migrated – for no known cause – to Mytilene on the nearby island of Lesbos. It is supposed that he there met Theophrastus, a native of Eresus on the same island, who was to become his pupil, his colleague, and his intellectual heir. Later, and again for unknown reasons, Aristotle left

3. Hermias gave Aristotle and his companions 'the city of Assos to live in;
and they spent their time there in philosophy, meeting together in a
courtyard, and Hermias provided them with all they needed'. The
courtyard has vanished; parts of the later city wall still stand.

the Aegean to return to his birthplace of Stagira, where he remained until he answered Philip's royal summons.

Hermias received a bad press in antiquity: he was not only a tyrant – he was also a barbarian, and a eunuch. But he served Aristotle generously. In return, Aristotle married his niece, Pythias, who was the mother of his two children, Pythias and Nicomachus; and when, in 341, Hermias was betrayed, tortured, and put to death in grisly fashion by the Persians, Aristotle composed in his memory a hymn to virtue. Whatever the character of Hermias may have been, science is in his debt. For it was during Aristotle's years of travel, between 347 and 335, and in particular during his stay in the eastern Aegean, that he undertook the major part of the work on which his scientific reputation rests.

For if Aristotle's historical researches are impressive, they are nothing compared to his work in the natural sciences. He made or collected observations in astronomy, meteorology, chemistry, physics, psychology, and half a dozen other sciences; but his scientific fame rests primarily on his work in zoology and biology: his studies on animals laid the foundations of the biological sciences; and they were not superseded until more than two millennia after his death. Some considerable part of the enquiries upon which those studies are based was carried out in Assos and on Lesbos; at all events, the place-names which from time to time punctuate Aristotle's remarks on marine biology point to the eastern Aegean as a main area of research.

The facts which Aristotle so assiduously uncovered were displayed in two large volumes, the *History of Animals* and the *Dissections*. The *Dissections* has not survived. It was concerned, as its name implies, with the internal parts and structure of animals; and there is reason to believe that it contained – or perhaps largely consisted of – diagrams and drawings. The *History of Animals* has survived. Its title (like the titles of several Aristotelian works) is misleading: the word 'history'

ΘΕΩΦΡΑΣΤοC

ΜΕΛΑΝΤΑ

ΕΡΕΣΙΩC

THEOPHRASTUS.

In ædibus Marchionis F. de Maximis in marmore.

4. 'Aristotle . . . then migrated to Mytilene on the nearby island of Lesbos. It is supposed that he there met Theophrastus, a native of Eresus on the same island, who was to become his pupil, colleague, and intellectual heir.'

transliterates the Greek word '*historia*' which means 'enquiry' or 'research', and a better translation of the title would be *Zoological Researches*.

The *History* – the *Researches* – discusses in detail the parts of animals, both external and internal; the different stuffs – blood, bone, hair, and the rest – of which animal bodies are constructed; the various modes of reproduction found among animals; their diet, habitat, and behaviour. Aristotle talks of sheep, goats, deer, pigs, lions, hyenas, elephants, camels, mice, mules. He describes swallows, pigeons, quails, woodpeckers, eagles, crows, blackbirds, cuckoos. His researches cover tortoises and lizards, crocodiles and vipers, porpoises and whales. He goes through the kinds of insect. And he is particularly informed and particularly informative about marine animals – fish, crustacea, cephalopods, testacea. The *Researches* ranges from man to the cheese-mite, from the European bison to the Mediterranean oyster. Every species of animal known to the Greeks is noticed; most species are given detailed descriptions; in some cases Aristotle's accounts are both long and accurate.

Zoology was a new science: where should Aristotle, confronted with such a vast variety of animal life, make a start? This is his answer:

> First, let us consider the parts of men; for just as people test currency by referring it to the standard most familiar to them, so it is in other cases too – and men are of necessity the sort of animal most familiar to us. Now the parts of men are clear enough to perception; nevertheless, in order that we may not break the proper sequence, and in order that we may rely on reason as well as perception, we must describe their parts – first the organic parts, then the uniform parts. Now the chief parts into which the body as a whole divides are these: head, neck, torso, two arms, two legs.

Aristotle begins with men, because men are most familiar, and can be used as a reference point. Much of what he says will, he is aware, be perfectly well known – it may seem childish or pedantic to record that men have necks between their heads and torsos. But Aristotle wants to give a full and orderly account, even at the cost of occasional banality; and in any event, the discussion quickly becomes more professional. The following passage will give some flavour of the *Researches*.

The octopus uses its tentacles both as feet and as hands: it draws in food with the two that are placed over its mouth; and the last of its tentacles, which is very pointed and the only one of them which is whitish and bifurcated at the tip (it uncoils towards the *rhachis* – the *rhachis* is the smooth surface on the opposite side from the suckers) – this it uses for copulation. In front of the sac and above the tentacles it has a hollow tube by which it discharges the sea-water which gets into the sac whenever it takes anything in with its mouth. It moves this tube to right and to left; and it discharges milt through it. It swims obliquely in the direction of the so-called head, stretching out its feet; and when it swims in this way it can see forwards (since its eyes are on top) and has its mouth at the rear. As long as the animal is alive, its head is hard and as it were inflated. It grasps and retains things with the underside of its tentacles, and the membrane between its feet is fully extended. If it gets on to the sand, it can no longer retain its hold.

Aristotle goes on to discuss the size of the tentacles. He compares the octopus to the other cephalopods – cuttlefish, crayfish, and the like. He gives a detailed description of the internal organs of the creature, which he had evidently dissected and examined with some attention. In the passage I have quoted he refers to the phenomenon known as 'hectocotylization' – the bifurcation in one of the tentacles of the male octopus, by means of which it copulates with the female. The phenomenon is not readily observed, and Aristotle himself was not entirely certain of it (at any rate, elsewhere he expresses doubt as to whether the octopus really uses a tentacle for copulation); but his remarks are entirely correct, and the facts which he reports were not rediscovered until the middle of the nineteenth century.

It is easy to become starry-eyed over the *Researches*, which are on any account a work of genius and a monument of indefatigable industry. Unsurprisingly, killjoy scholars have felt obliged to point out the several deficiencies of the work.

First of all, Aristotle is accused of frequent and crude error. A notorious example again concerns copulation. Aristotle asserts more than once that during copulation the female fly inserts a tube or filament upwards into the male – and he says that 'this is plain to anyone who tries to separate copulating flies'. It is not plain: on the contrary, Aristotle's assertion is false. Another example concerns the European bison. After a vague description of the shaggy beast, Aristotle observes that it is regularly hunted for its meat, and that 'it defends itself by kicking, and by excreting and discharging its excrement over a distance of eight yards – it can do this easily and often, and the excrement burns so much that it scalds the hair of the hounds'. A splendid picture, and apparently told without tongue in cheek: Aristotle was taken in by a tipsy huntsman's after-dinner yarn.

Secondly, Aristotle is charged with failing to use 'the experimental method'. The observations which fill his works – observations made by others or made by himself – are, most of them, amateur. They were made in the field and not in the laboratory. Aristotle never attempted to establish appropriate experimental conditions or to make controlled observations. There is no evidence that he tried to repeat observations, to check them, or to verify them. His whole procedure was, by any scientific standards, slapdash.

Thirdly, Aristotle is criticized for having no notion of the importance of measurement. Real science is quantitative: Aristotle's descriptions are qualitative. He was no mathematician. He had no notion of applying mathematics to zoology. He did not weigh or measure his specimens. He records a layman's impression of how things look rather than a professional's calculation of how they are.

There is some truth in all these charges – Aristotle was not infallible, and he was a pioneer. But the charges are misplaced. The first is unexciting. There are numerous mistakes in the *Researches*, some to be explained by the fact that Aristotle possessed few technical instruments and some to be set down as plain errors of observation or judgement. (His most influential error gave rise to the theory of 'spontaneous generation'. Some insects, Aristotle asserts, 'are generated not from parent creatures but spontaneously: some from the dew that falls on leaves . . . some in mud and dung when they putrefy, some in wood (either on plants or in dead wood), some in the hair of animals, some in animals' flesh, some in their excrement'. Aristotle had observed lice on the head and worms in dung; but, for want of care or for want of instruments, he had not observed the phenomena with sufficient accuracy.) But the errors are greatly outnumbered by the insights – and what scientific work has ever been free of error?

The *Researches* contains one passage which is often said to report an experiment. Aristotle is describing the early development of chicks in the egg. He records in considerable detail the stage of growth reached by the embryo on successive days: he removed one egg a day from the clutch under the brooding hen, he cracked it open, and he chronicled the daily changes. (If we are to believe the implications of the text, he did this not only for the domestic hen – the case he describes in detail – but also for other birds.)

The description of the chicken embryo is one of the more remarkable passages in the *Researches*; but it is not the report of an experiment. (For example, Aristotle, so far as we know, did not control the conditions in which the eggs were incubated.) Nor is it typical of the

Researches as a whole, where such dated and consecutive observations are rare. But this is hardly odd. The 'experimental method' is of no particular importance to the sort of research that Aristotle was engaged upon. He was inaugurating a new science. There was a superabundance of information waiting to be collected, sifted, recorded, and systematized. Experimental evidence was not required. Nor, in any case, is experiment appropriate in descriptive zoology. You do not need the 'experimental method' to determine that men have two legs or to describe the hectocotylization of the octopus. Aristotle himself was aware that different sciences call for different methods. Those who accuse him of failing to experiment are victims of the vulgar error that all the sciences must be approached by the experimental path.

It is sometimes said in reply to the third charge that Aristotle's zoology is non-quantitative because he did not possess the technical devices upon which quantitative science relies: he had no thermometer, no finely calibrated scales, no accurate chronometer. That is all true; but the point should not be exaggerated. Greek shopkeepers weighed and measured dead meat, and there was no technical reason why Aristotle should not have weighed and measured it live. Nor is it relevant to observe that Aristotle was no mathematician. Although he did not himself contribute to mathematical progress, he was well acquainted with the work of his contemporaries (mathematical examples and references are common enough in his writings); and in any case it requires little mathematical expertise to introduce measurement into science.

The *Researches* does, in fact, contain plenty of indeterminately quantitative statements (this animal is larger than that, this creature emits more semen than the other). There are also a few determinately quantitative observations. Of the two main types of squid, Aristotle remarks that 'the so-called *teuthoi* are much larger than the *teuthides*, growing to a length of up to seven and a half feet; some cuttlefish have

22

been found three feet long, and the tentacles of the octopus sometimes reach that size or even longer'. Aristotle seems to have measured the cephalopods. He could well have weighed them and given their other vital statistics, but he chose not to do so. And that was not an error but a wise choice. As Aristotle clearly saw, it is form and function rather than weight and size which matter in his kind of zoology. The length of an octopus' tentacles, which varies from specimen to specimen, is of little scientific interest; it is with the structure of the tentacles, and, with their functional role in the animal's life, that the scientist is concerned.

The *Researches* is not flawless, but it is a masterpiece. Nowhere else does Aristotle show more vividly his 'desire to know'.

Chapter 4
Collecting Facts

Aristotle was a research scientist, and much of his time was devoted to original and first-hand study: he recorded his own observations, and he carried out dissections himself. But he could not have based all his multifarious descriptions on personal research, and like any other seeker after knowledge he borrowed other men's observations and culled other men's flowers. What, then, were Aristotle's research methods? How did he approach his work?

A pleasant story has it that Alexander the Great, 'inflamed by a desire to know the natures of animals', arranged for 'several thousand men throughout the whole of Greece and Asia Minor to be at Aristotle's disposal – everyone who lived by hunting or falconry or fishing, or who looked after parks, herds, apiaries, fishponds, or aviaries – so that no living creature should escape his notice'. It is unlikely that Alexander ever did anything of the sort; but behind the story lies the fact that in the *Researches* Aristotle makes frequent reference to the reports of beekeepers and fishermen, of hunters and herdsmen, of all those engaged in agriculture and animal husbandry. Beekeepers are experienced in the ways of bees, and Aristotle relied on their expertise. Fishermen see things which landlubbers never observe, and Aristotle sought information from them. He was properly cautious in using their information. Some people, he says, deny that fish copulate; but they are wrong. 'Their error is made easier by the fact that such fish copulate quickly, so that even many fishermen fail to observe it – for none of them observes this sort of thing for the sake of knowledge.' Nevertheless, much of Aristotle's work is based partly on the testimony of such professionals.

In addition, Aristotle had written sources at his disposal. The Greek doctors had made some study of human anatomy, and Aristotle uses their writings in his treatment of the parts of men – his detailed account of the vascular system includes long quotations from three of his predecessors. In general, Aristotle's researches included a comprehensive programme of reading: 'he worked so hard . . . that his house was called the House of the Reader'. And he had a large library: 'he is the first man we know to have collected books, and his example taught the Kings of Egypt how to put together a library'.

For Aristotle's zoological researches book learning was of limited importance, for there were few books from which he could learn. But in other disciplines there was much to peruse. Aristotle recommends that 'one should make excerpts from written accounts, making lists separately for each subject, e.g. for the good, or for animals', and the catalogue of his books shows that he himself prepared various compilations of that sort. Many of his own discussions begin with a brief history of the question at issue, setting out in summary form the opinions which his predecessors had advanced. When discussing the nature and variety of causes in the *Metaphysics* he observes that

> we have given sufficient consideration to this subject in the *Physics*;
> nevertheless, let us also set down the views of those who have
> preceded us in the enquiry into existing things and in the philosophical
> investigation of reality; for it is plain that they too say that there are
> certain principles and causes. And this, as we proceed, will be useful to
> our present enquiry; for either we shall find some further kind of cause
> or else we shall be more firmly convinced about those we have just
> mentioned.

Aristotle wrote several essays in intellectual history. His early work *On Philosophy* contained a full account of the origins and development of the subject; and there were monographs on Pythagoras, on Democritus, on Alcmaeon, and others. Only fragments of these works have survived; but the summary histories in the treatises no doubt drew upon them. Judged purely as intellectual history these summaries are not beyond criticism (and modern scholars have sometimes flayed them); but such criticism is beside the point: the purpose of the summaries was not to chronicle the history of an idea; it was to provide a starting-point for Aristotle's own investigations and to serve as a check upon his own speculations.

There were not always past enquiries to consult. At the end of one of his logical treatises, Aristotle writes that

> in the case of rhetoric there was much old material to hand, but in the case of logic we had absolutely nothing at all until we had spent a long time in laborious investigation. If, when you consider the matter and remember the state from which we began, you think that the subject is now sufficiently advanced compared to those other disciplines which have developed in the course of tradition, then it remains for all of you who have heard our lectures to forgive our omissions and to thank us warmly for our discoveries.

The note of self-satisfaction is not typical of Aristotle, even if he fully deserves his pat on the back. But I cite the passage to show, by implicit contrast, that Aristotle's customary procedure was to build upon the work of his predecessors. He could not do that in logic; and he could do it only to a limited extent in biology. In other subjects, 'which have developed in the course of tradition', he gratefully accepted everything which the tradition offered him.

Reliance on tradition, or the use of past discoveries, is a prudent procedure – an indispensable procedure – for any scientific enquirer.

5. Teacher and pupils: a relief from the second century AC. Aristotle believed that knowledge and teaching were inseparable'.

But in Aristotle the matter goes a little deeper. He was highly conscious of his own position at the end of a long line of thinkers; he had a strong sense of intellectual history and of his own place therein. And his advice to attend to reputable opinions is more than a prudent suggestion: after all, men desire by nature to discover the truth; nature would not have given men such a desire and left its satisfaction impossible; and consequently, if men generally believe something, then that is a sign that it is more likely to be true than false.

This Aristotelian conviction bears directly upon two characteristic features of his thought. First, he insists on the value of what he calls 'reputable opinions'. Something believed by all or most men – at any rate by all or most clever men – is thereby 'reputable'; and it must, so Aristotle thinks, have something to be said in its favour. In the *Topics*, a work primarily concerned with reasoning from and about 'reputable opinions', he advises us to collect such opinions and to use them as starting-points for our enquiries. In the *Nicomachean Ethics* he implies that, in practical philosophy at least, reputable opinions are the end-points as well as the starting-points: 'for if the difficulties are solved and the reputable opinions remain, sufficient proof of the matter will have been given'. In our ethical investigations we shall make a collection of the pertinent 'reputable opinions'; we shall winnow them to blow out the chaff of falsity; and what is left on the floor, the grains of truth, constitutes the result and sum of our enquiry.

Secondly, Aristotle had a clear idea of the importance of tradition in the growth of knowledge.

> In all cases of discovery, when work is taken over from others who have earlier laboured on the matter, gradual progress is later made by the hands of those who have taken it over, whereas what is discovered at the very beginning customarily makes but little advance at first. And yet this is far more useful than the later increase which depends upon it. For the beginning is doubtless the most important thing of all, as they

say. And that is why it is hardest; for the greater it is in power, the smaller it is in magnitude and the harder to see. But once it is discovered, it is relatively easy to add to and increase the rest.

Or again:

Investigation of reality is in a way difficult, in a way easy. An indication of this is that no one can attain it in a wholly satisfactory way, and that no one misses it completely: each of us says *something* about nature, and although as individuals we advance the subject little if at all, from all of us taken together something of size results – and, as the proverb has it, who can miss a barn-door? . . . And it is fair to thank not only those whose beliefs we share, but also those whose views were more superficial; for they too contributed something – for they prepared things for us. If Timotheus had not existed, we should lack a great deal of lyric poetry; but if Phrynis had not existed, Timotheus would not have done so. It is the same with those who have expressed views on reality. For from some we have taken over certain opinions, and others were the causes of the existence of those men.

The acquisition of knowledge is arduous, and science grows slowly. The first step is the hardest, for then we have nothing to guide our journey. Later, the labour is lighter; but even so, as individuals we can contribute little to the growing pile of knowledge; it is collectively that the ants amass their anthill.

Chapter 5
The Philosophical
Background

Aristotle was an indefatigable collector of facts – facts zoological, astronomical, meteorological, historical, sociological. Some of his political researches were carried out during the final period of his life when, from 335 to 322, he taught at the Lyceum in Athens; much of his biological research was done during the years of travel, between 347 and 335. There is reason to believe that his collecting activities were just as brisk during the first period of his adult life, the years between 367 and 347: that period is yet to be described.

So far, we have seen Aristotle as a public figure and as a private researcher; but that is at most half the man. Aristotle, after all, is reputed to have been a philosopher, and there is nothing very philosophical about the jackdaw operations I have so far described. Indeed, one of Aristotle's ancient enemies accused him of being a mere jackdaw:

> why did he turn away from exhorting the young and incur the terrible wrath and enmity both of the followers of Isocrates and of some other sophists? He must surely have implanted a great admiration for his powers, from the moment when he abandoned his proper business and was found, together with his pupil, collecting laws and innumerable constitutions and legal pleas about territory and appeals based on circumstances and everything of that sort, choosing . . . to know and

teach philosophy and rhetoric and politics and agriculture and cosmetics and mining – and the trades performed by those who are ashamed of what they are doing and say they practise them from necessity.

The accusation is puffed up with rhetoric and contains some absurd falsifications: Aristotle never devoted much study to cosmetics. But it is worth pondering. Aristotle's studies in 'politics and agriculture' are impressive, the *Constitutions* and the *Researches* are magnificent works; but how are they connected with *philosophy*?

Aristotle was born in 384, in the northern Greek town of Stagira. His father died when Aristotle was still young, and he was brought up by his uncle Proxenus, who had connections with Atarneus. Nothing is recorded about Aristotle's early education; but since he came from a rich and learned family, he no doubt received the sort of literary and gymnastic training which was normal for a well born Greek. In 367, at the age of seventeen, he left Stagira for Athens, where he joined the brilliant group of men who worked and studied in the Academy under the leadership of Plato. In one of his lost works Aristotle told how a Corinthian farmer had happened to read Plato's *Gorgias* and 'at once gave up his farm and his vines, mortgaged his soul to Plato, and sowed and planted it with Plato's philosophy'. Is that fictionalized autobiography? Perhaps the young Aristotle read Plato's dialogues in Stagira and was seduced by Dame Philosophy. However that may be, the move to Athens and the Academy was the crucial event in Aristotle's career.

The Academy, like the Lyceum, was a public place, and Plato's school was no more a modern university than was Aristotle's. Yet there were some differences between the two establishments. Plato owned a private estate near the Academy. His lectures and discussions were not, as a rule, public. Indeed, Plato's school appears to have been a fairly exclusive club. In 367 Aristotle took out membership.

6. A mosaic from Pompeii, made in about 100 BC, showing Plato's Academy. 'The Academy was primarily a school of philosophy . . . Plato encouraged other men's researches in other subjects, and he gathered about him the most talented minds in Greece.'

Plato himself was no polymath. He did not pretend to the range
which his most famous pupil was to attain. Rather, his own researches
were more or less limited to the areas which we today think of as
peculiarly philosophical – metaphysics, the theory of knowledge,
logic, ethics, political theory. The Academy was primarily a school
of philosophy. Not that Plato was blinkered. He encouraged other
men's researches in other subjects, and he gathered about him
the most talented minds in Greece. Mathematics was certainly
studied in the Academy. Plato, himself no mathematician, was
keenly interested in the methods of mathematics; he set his
pupils mathematical problems and he urged them to study the
mathematical sciences. It is probable that natural science too was
studied. Plato's *Timaeus* contains speculation of a scientific nature,
and a comic dramatist guyed the young Academicians thus: 'In the
gymnasium of the Academy I heard some absurd and extraordinary
arguments. They were discussing nature, and distinguishing sorts
of animal, and kinds of tree, and species of vegetable – and then
they tried to discover to what species the pumpkin belongs.' Plato
was interested in problems of classification; and those problems
had some bearing upon Aristotle's later attempts at biological
taxonomy.

Again, the Academy found a place for rhetoric. It was in that subject
that Aristotle first made a name for himself. In about 360 he wrote a
dialogue, the *Gryllus*, on the subject of rhetoric, in which he attacked
the views of Isocrates, a leading rhetorician, a public educator and a
professional pundit. The attack provoked a riposte, and the quarrel
ranged far beyond the domain of rhetorical theory. One of Isocrates'
pupils, Cephisodorus, replied to the *Gryllus* with a long counterblast,
the first of many polemics to be directed against Aristotle.
(Cephisodorus accused Aristotle of wasting his time in collecting
proverbs – evidence that by 360 Aristotle had already begun his
compilatory activities.) Some years later, in his *Protrepticus*, Aristotle
returned to the fray, defending the ideals of the Academy against the

more pragmatic notions of Isocrates' school. Isocrates himself replied in his *Antidosis*.

The squabble with the Isocrateans did not imply a rejection of rhetoric itself, which continued to interest Aristotle. (And let it be noted that Aristotle was honest and generous enough to praise Isocrates' literary style.) The first drafts of his treatise on *Rhetoric*, which, unlike the *Gryllus* and the *Protrepticus*, still survives intact, may well go back to those early years in the Academy; and the final touches were not put to the work until the latest period of his life. Rhetoric and the study of literature are closely connected: Aristotle wrote a historico-critical book *On the Poets* and a collection of *Homeric Problems*. Those studies too may have been undertaken in the Academy. They showed Aristotle to be a serious student of philology and of literary criticism, and they doubtless formed part of the preparatory work for the third book of the *Rhetoric*, which is a treatise on language and style, and for the *Poetics*, in which Aristotle elaborated his account of the nature of tragic drama.

Rhetoric is also connected with logic – indeed, one of Aristotle's main claims in the *Gryllus* was that an orator should not excite the passions by fine language but rather persuade the reason by fine argument. Plato himself was greatly interested in logic, or 'dialectic' as it was called; and the Academicians indulged in a sort of intellectual gymnastics in which set theses were to be defended and attacked by means of a variety of stylized arguments. Aristotle's *Topics* was first outlined in his Academic years. The work lists and comments upon various general forms of argument which the young gymnasts were encouraged to use. (The Greek word '*topos*', in one of its uses, means something like 'form of argument' – hence the curious title, *Topics*.) The *Sophistical Refutations*, an appendix to the *Topics*, catalogues a variety of fallacies, some silly and others profound, which the gymnasts had to recognize and to resolve.

Aristotle remained in Athens as a member of Plato's Academy for twenty years. In 347, the year in which Plato died, he left Athens for Atarneus: he was thirty-seven, a philosopher and a scientist in his own right. What, in those two formative decades, did he learn? What aspects of Academic philosophy influenced him and gave shape to his own later views?

He loved Plato, and on his death wrote an elegy in which he praised him as a man 'whom it is not right for evil men even to praise; who alone or first of mortals proved clearly, by his own life and by the course of his arguments, that a man becomes good and happy at the same time'. But you may love a man while rejecting his beliefs. Aristotle was no Platonist. Many of the doctrines central to Platonism are strongly criticized in Aristotle's treatises, and he criticized Plato during his lifetime. 'Plato used to call Aristotle the Foal. What did he mean by the name? Clearly it was known that foals kick their mothers when they have had enough milk.' Ancient critics accused the Foal of ingratitude, but the charge is absurd – no teacher requires his pupils to subscribe to his own doctrines from a sense of gratitude. Moreover, whether or not Aristotle ever accepted any of Plato's central theories, he was certainly profoundly influenced by them. I shall pick out five points which together determined much of Aristotle's philosophical thought, and turned him into a philosophical scientist rather than a mere collector of agricultural information.

First of all, Plato had reflected on the unity of the sciences. He saw human knowledge as a potentially unified system: science, for him, was not the random amassing of facts; it was the organization of facts into a coherent account of the world. Aristotle, too, was a systematic thinker, and he shared wholeheartedly in Plato's vision of a unified theory of science, even if he disagreed with Plato about the way in which that unity was to be achieved and exhibited.

Secondly, Plato was a dialectician. Aristotle claims to have been a pioneer in the science of logic, and it is indisputable that Aristotle

7. Head of Plato, 'whom it is not right for evil men even to praise; who alone or first of mortals proved clearly, by his own life and by the course of his arguments, that a man becomes good and happy at the same time.'

turned logic into a science and invented the discipline of formal logic – Aristotle, not Plato, was the first logician. But Plato, both in his dialogues – most notably in the *Parmenides* and the *Sophist* – and in the dialectical exercises he encouraged in the Academy, had prepared the ground for Aristotle. He had initiated enquiry into some of the foundations of logic (for example, into the structure of propositions); and he had expected his pupils to train themselves in the practice of argumentation.

Again, Plato was concerned with problems of ontology. ('Ontology' is a grandiose name for a part of metaphysics: an ontologist attempts to determine what sort of things really exist, what are the fundamental entities of which the world consists.) Plato's ontology was contained in his theory of Ideas or Forms. According to that theory, the ultimate realities – the things on which the reality of everything else is somehow dependent – are abstract universals. It is not individual men and individual horses – Tom, Dick, and Harry; Surrey, Barbary, and Bucephalus – but the abstract forms of Man or manhood and of Horse or horseness which constitute the basic furniture of the real world. The theory is not easy to understand, let alone to accept. Aristotle did not accept it (and, some have thought, did not understand it); but it gnawed at him throughout his philosophical career, and it directed his own numerous (and often baffling) efforts to develop an alternative ontology.

Fourthly, Plato thought of scientific knowledge as a search for the causes or explanations of things. In his view, the notions of science and knowledge were intimately tied to that of explanation, and he discussed the types of explanation that might be given and the conditions under which phenomena could and should be explained. Aristotle inherited that concern. He too ties knowledge to explanation. His scientific endeavours were directed not merely to observing and recording, but above all to explaining.

Finally, the notion of knowledge itself raises certain philosophical questions: What is it to know something? How can we acquire knowledge, or by what channels do we come to understand the world? Why suppose, indeed, that we know anything at all? The part of philosophy which deals with such questions is customarily called epistemology ('*epistêmê*' is the Greek for 'knowledge'). Epistemology matters to any philosopher who is concerned with science and the sciences; and epistemological theories will be determined, in part at least, by issues in ontology. Many passages in Plato's dialogues are given to epistemological discussion. Here, too, Aristotle followed in his master's footsteps.

Knowledge must be systematic and unified. Its structure is given by logic, and its unity rests at bottom on ontology. It is essentially explanatory. It poses deep philosophical problems. All that, and much more, Aristotle learned in the Academy. However profoundly he disagreed with Plato's detailed elaboration of those five issues, he was at one with Plato in principle. In the next few chapters I shall sketch Aristotle's views on these subjects. By the end of the sketch it will be possible to see why Aristotle is much more than a collector of facts – why he is a philosopher-scientist.

Chapter 6
The Structure of the Sciences

The most developed of Greek sciences was geometry – indeed, for centuries, Euclid's name was synonymous with the science of geometry. Although Euclid's work was done after Aristotle's death, Euclid built on the researches of his predecessors, and those predecessors had given some thought to what was to become the distinctive feature of Euclid's own geometrical science. In a word, Euclid's geometry is an axiomatized deductive system: he selects a few simple principles, or axioms, which he posits as the primary truths of his subject; and from those axioms he derives, by a series of logically compelling deductions, all the other truths of geometry. Geometry thus consists of derived truths, or theorems, and primary truths, or axioms. Each theorem follows logically – though often by way of a long and complex chain of reasoning   from one or more of the axioms.

The notion of an axiomatic deductive system is elegant and intellectually attractive. Plato was attracted to it, and he suggested that the whole of human knowledge might somehow be set out in a single axiomatized system: from a small set of primary truths, every other scientific truth might be logically deduced. Knowledge is thus systematic and unitary – it is systematic because it can be presented axiomatically, unitary because all truths can be derived from a single set of axioms.

Aristotle was no less impressed than Plato by the power of axiomatization, but he did not believe Plato's optimistic claim that all knowledge could be founded upon a single set of axioms. For he was equally impressed by the apparent independence of the sciences. Mathematicians and doctors, biologists and physicists, work in different domains, discuss different objects, and follow different methods. Their disciplines rarely overlap. Nevertheless, Aristotle felt the need for system: if human knowledge is not unitary, neither is it a mere disconnected plurality. 'The causes and principles of different things are different – in one way; but in another way, if you speak universally and by analogy, they are all the same.' The axioms of geometry and the principles of biology are mutually independent, but they are the same 'by analogy': that is to say, the conceptual apparatus and the formal structure of all the sciences are the same.

Aristotle divided knowledge into three major classes: 'all thought is either practical or productive or theoretical'. The productive sciences are those concerned with the making of things – cosmetics and farming, art and engineering. Aristotle himself had relatively little to say about productive knowledge. The *Rhetoric* and the *Poetics* are his only surviving exercises in that area. (*Poetics* in Greek is '*poiêtikê*', and that is the word translated as 'productive' in the phrase 'the productive sciences'.) The practical sciences are concerned with action, or more precisely with how we ought to act in various circumstances, in private and in public affairs. The *Ethics* and the *Politics* are Aristotle's chief contributions to the practical sciences.

Knowledge is theoretical when its goal is neither production nor action but simply truth. Theoretical knowledge includes all that we now think of as science, and in Aristotle's view it contained by far the greatest part of the sum of human knowledge. It subdivides into three species: 'there are three theoretical philosophies – mathematics, natural science, and theology'. Aristotle was intimately acquainted with contemporary mathematics, as any student of Plato's would be, and

Books XIII and XIV of the *Metaphysics* are acute essays on the nature of numbers; but he was not a professional mathematician and did not pretend to have advanced the subject.

Natural science includes botany, zoology, psychology, meteorology, chemistry, physics. (The term I translate as 'natural science' is '*phusikê*', often misleadingly transliterated as 'physics'. Aristotle's *Physics* is a treatise about natural science as such.) Aristotle thinks that the objects of natural science are marked off by two characteristics: they are capable of change or motion (unlike the objects of mathematics) and they exist 'separately' or in their own right. (The second point will be examined in a later chapter.) The greater part of Aristotle's life was devoted to the study of such objects.

Nevertheless, natural science is not the best of sciences. 'If there are no substances apart from natural substances, natural science will be the primary science; but if there are changeless substances, the science of them will be prior and will be the primary philosophy'. Aristotle agreed with Plato that there are such changeless substances, and he called such substances divine. Their study may thus be called theology, or the science of things divine. Theology is superior to natural science: 'the theoretical sciences are preferable to the rest, and this to the other theoretical sciences'. But the term 'theology' should be construed carefully: I shall say a little about Aristotle's divinities in a later chapter; here it is enough to observe that he usually identifies them with parts of the heavens, so that 'theology' might well seem to be a branch of astronomy.

Two things for which Aristotle cared greatly appear to have escaped the net: metaphysics and logic. Where are they to be placed in the system of the sciences? Both seem to be theoretical, and both are treated by Aristotle as in some way identical with theology.

According to Aristotle, 'there is a science which studies beings *qua* being and the things that belong to them in their own right'. (This science is often identified as metaphysics, or at least as a chief part of metaphysics, and Aristotle studies it in his *Metaphysics*. But Aristotle never uses the term 'metaphysics', and the title '*Metaphysics*' means literally 'What comes after natural science'.) The phrase 'beings *qua* being' has a pleasantly esoteric ring to it, and many scholars have supposed it to denote some abstruse and abstract item. (The supposition is aided by a common mistranslation of the Aristotelian formula which renders it in the singular, as 'being *qua* being'.) In fact Aristotle means something neither abstract nor abstruse. 'Beings *qua* being' are not a special class or kind of being; indeed, there are no such things as beings-*qua*-being at all. When Aristotle says that there is a science which studies beings *qua* being, he means that there is a science which studies beings, and studies them *qua* being; that is to say, there is a science which studies the things that exist (and not some abstract item called 'being'), and studies them *qua* existing.

The little word '*qua*' plays an important role in Aristotle's philosophy. There is nothing mysterious about it. Pooh-Bah, in *The Mikado*, is, among other things, Chancellor of the Exchequer and Private Secretary to Ko-Ko. He has different attitudes in his different capacities. As Chancellor, he urges a frugal wedding ceremony for Ko-Ko and his bride; as Secretary, he recommends a splurge. He does one thing *qua* Chancellor or under his Chancellor's hat, another *qua* Secretary or under his Secretarial hat. In the former case the cares of State are relevant to his advice, in the latter his recommendation is determined by different considerations. Similarly, to study something *qua* existent is to study just those features of the thing which are relevant to its *existing* – and not any of the many other features of the thing; it is to study it under its existential hat. Everyone who does not study fictions studies 'beings', things that exist; the student of beings *qua* being studies just those aspects of existent things which belong to them in virtue of the fact that they exist.

The study of beings *qua* being is thus supremely general: everything that exists falls within its purview (contrast entomology or phonology, which are restricted to insects and to linguistic sounds), and the properties it investigates are those which absolutely everything must have. (Thus Book X of the *Metaphysics* discusses what it is to be *one* thing. *Everything* is *one* thing; by contrast, only some things are monopterous or consonantal.) Aristotle engages in this highly general study in various books of the *Metaphysics*. Several of his logical writings, both extant and lost, were also devoted to it.

Now this general study of beings *qua* being is, in Aristotle's view, the primary philosophy, and hence it is identified with theology. This is odd: how, we may wonder, can a science which studies absolutely everything be the same as a science which studies only a special and highly privileged class of things? Aristotle anticipated the question. He suggests that theology 'is universal because it is primary'; and he appears to mean that if you study the primary substances on which all other entities are dependent, then you will implicitly be studying *all* existents *qua* existent. Not everyone has found that suggestion compelling, and Aristotle's primary philosophy is sometimes thought to consist of two quite distinct parts, a general metaphysics which studies beings *qua* being, and a special metaphysics which studies the principles and causes of things.

As to logic, later philosophers disputed its status and its position among the sciences. Some held that logic was a 'part' of philosophy – a discipline to be set alongside mathematics and natural science. Others, including Aristotle's own followers, urged that logic was a 'tool' of philosophy – something which was used by philosophers and scientists but did not qualify as an object of their studies in its own right. (The Greek for 'tool' is '*organon*': that is why later Aristotelians gave the collective title *Organon* to Aristotle's logical writings.) Other philosophers claimed, more plausibly, that logic is both a part and a tool of philosophy.

8. 'Aristotle himself did not discuss the position of logic in his scheme of things.' In the Renaissance it was sometimes imagined as the tap-root of the tree of knowledge in Aristotle's philosophical garden.

Aristotle himself did not discuss the position of logic in his scheme of things. He argues that the student of beings *qua* being will study 'the things which the mathematicians call axioms' or 'the first principles of deduction'; 'for they belong to everything that exists, and not to some particular kind of thing separately from the others'. And he holds that the logician 'assumes the same form as the philosopher' or discusses the same range of things as the student of primary philosophy. After all, logic, being an entirely general science, should presumably be subsumed under metaphysics or the science of beings *qua* being. But there are passages in which Aristotle seems to imply that logic is not to be so categorized; and indeed, having said that the logician 'assumes the same form as the philosopher', he immediately adds that he nevertheless follows a distinct profession.

The structure of human knowledge, as Aristotle regarded it, can be exhibited in a diagram, thus:

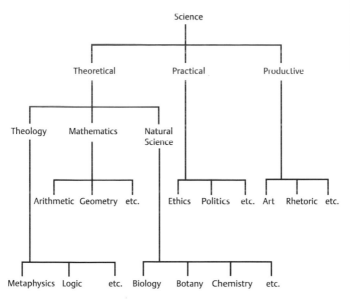

Chapter 7
Logic

The sciences – at any rate the theoretical sciences – are to be axiomatized. What, then, are their axioms to be? What conditions must a proposition satisfy to count as an axiom? Again, what form will the derivations within each science take? By what rules will theorems be deduced from axioms? Those are among the questions which Aristotle poses in his logical writings, and in particular in the works known as the *Prior* and *Posterior Analytics*. Let us first look at the rules for deduction, and thus at the formal part of Aristotle's logic. 'All sentences are meaningful . . . but not all make statements: only those in which truth and falsity are found do so.' 'Of statements, some are simple, that is, those which affirm or deny something of something, and others are composed of these, and are thereby compound sentences.' As a logician, Aristotle is interested only in sentences that are true and false (commands, questions, exhortations, and the like are the concern of the student of rhetoric or linguistics). He holds that every such sentence is either simple or else compounded from simple sentences; and he explains that simple sentences are those which affirm or deny something of something – some *one* thing of some *one* thing, as he later insists.

In the *Prior Analytics* Aristotle uses the word 'proposition' for simple sentences and the word 'term' for their salient parts. Thus a proposition affirms or denies something of something, and the two things are its terms. The thing affirmed or denied is called the predicate of the proposition, and the thing of which the predicate is affirmed or denied is called the subject of the proposition. The propositions with which Aristotle's logic will concern itself are all either universal or particular; that is to say, they affirm or deny a predicate either of every item of some kind or of some item or items. Thus in the proposition 'Every viviparous animal is vertebrate', the word 'vertebrate' picks out the predicate and the phrase 'viviparous animal' picks out the subject; the proposition affirms the former of the latter – and of all the latter. Similarly, in the proposition 'Some oviparous animals are not sanguineous', 'sanguineous' picks out the predicate and 'oviparous animal' the subject, the proposition denying the former of some of the latter. It is easy to see that Aristotle's logic will concern itself with exactly four types of proposition: universal affirmatives, which affirm something of all of something; universal negatives, which deny something of all of something; particular affirmatives, which affirm something of some of something; and particular negatives, which deny something of some of something.

In addition, propositions come in a variety of moods: 'every proposition expresses either that something holds or that it necessarily holds or that it possibly holds'. Thus 'Some calamaries grow to a length of three feet' affirms that *being a yard long* actually holds true of some calamaries. 'Every man is necessarily constituted of flesh, bones, etc.' says that *being corporeal* holds necessarily of every man – that a thing could not be a man without being made of flesh, bones, etc. 'It is possible that no horses are asleep' states that *being asleep* possibly belongs to no horses – that every horse may be awake. These three moods or 'modalities' are called (though not by Aristotle) 'assertoric', 'apodeictic', and 'problematic'.

That, in brief, is Aristotle's account of the nature of propositions, as it is found in the *Analytics*. All propositions are simple or compounded of simples. Every simple proposition contains two terms, predicate and

9. 'A philosopher will surely be keen to secure axioms which are known and pertinent to the subject; for it is on these that scientific syllogisms are based' (*Topics*, 155b 14–16). The manuscript shown here was written by the monk Ephraim in November 954.

subject. Every simple proposition is either affirmative or negative. Every simple proposition is either universal or particular. Every simple proposition is either assertoric or apodeictic or problematic.

The doctrine of the *Analytics* is not quite the same as that of the short essay *On Interpretation*, a work in which Aristotle reflects at greater length on the nature and structure of simple propositions. And as a doctrine it is open to various objections. Are *all* propositions either simple or compounded from simples? For example, the sentence 'It is now recognized that the octopus' last tentacle is bifurcated' is surely compound – it contains as a part of itself the proposition 'the octopus' last tentacle is bifurcated'. But it is not compounded *from* simple propositions. It consists of a simple proposition prefixed by 'It is now recognized that', and 'It is now recognized that' is not a proposition. Again, do all simple propositions contain just two terms? 'It is raining' seems simple enough. But does it contain *two* terms? Again, what of the sentence 'Socrates is a man'? That surely contains a predicate and a subject. But it is neither universal nor particular – it does not say anything of 'all' or of 'some' Socrates; after all, the name 'Socrates' is not a general term, so that (as Aristotle himself observed) the phrases 'all' and 'some' do not apply to it.

Consider, finally, such sentences as 'Cows have four stomachs', 'Humans produce one offspring at a time', 'Stags shed their antlers annually' – sentences which make the very stuff of Aristotle's biological writings. It is not true that *every* cow has four stomachs – there are deformed specimens with three or five apiece. Yet Aristotle the biologist does not mean to say that *some* cows happen to have four stomachs, nor even that most cows do. Rather, he means to say that *every* cow naturally has four stomachs (even if, by some accident of birth, some cows in fact do not). Aristotle stresses that in nature many things hold 'for the most part', and he believes that most of the truths of the natural sciences will be expressible by way of sentences of the form 'By nature, every so-and-so is such-and-such', sentences which are true if for the most part so-and-so's are such-and-such. But what exactly is the structure of sentences of that form? Aristotle wrestled with the question, but he found no satisfactory answer.

The logical system which Aristotle develops in the *Prior Analytics* is based upon his account of the nature of propositions. The arguments he considers all consist of two premisses and one conclusion, each of these three components being a simple proposition. Logic is a general discipline, and Aristotle wanted to deal generally with all possible arguments (of the types he described). But there are indefinitely many arguments, and no treatise could possibly deal individually with all of them. In order to achieve generality, Aristotle introduced a simple device. Instead of employing particular terms – 'man', 'horse', 'swan' – in order to describe and characterize arguments, he used letters – A, B, C. Instead of genuine sentences, such as 'Every octopus has eight tentacles', he used quasi-sentences or sentence patterns, such as 'Every A is B.' This use of letters and sentence patterns allows Aristotle to speak with full generality; for what holds true of a pattern, holds true of every particular instance of the pattern. For example, Aristotle needs to show that from 'Some sea-creatures are mammals' we may infer 'Some mammals are sea-creatures', that from 'Some men are Greeks' we may infer 'Some Greeks are men', that from 'Some democracies are illiberal' we may infer 'Some illiberal regimes are democratic', and so on – he wants to show (as the jargon has it) that every particular affirmative proposition converts. He does so by considering the sentence pattern 'Some A is B', and by proving that from a sentence of that pattern we can infer the corresponding sentence of the pattern 'Some B is A'. If that has been shown to hold for the pattern, then it has been shown, at one blow, to hold for all of the indefinitely many instances of the pattern.

Aristotle invented this use of letters. Logicians are now so familiar with the invention, and employ it so unthinkingly, that they may forget how remarkable an invention it was. The *Prior Analytics* makes constant use of letters and patterns. Thus the very first type of argument which Aristotle describes and endorses is expressed by means of letters: 'If A is predicated of every B, and B of every C, necessarily A is predicated of every C'. In arguments of this form, all three propositions (the two premisses and the conclusion) are universal, affirmative, and assertoric. An instance might be: 'Every animal that breathes possesses lungs; every viviparous animal breathes; therefore every viviparous animal possesses lungs.'

In the first part of the *Prior Analytics* Aristotle considers all possible pairings of simple propositions, and determines from which pairs a third simple proposition may be inferred, and from which pairs no conclusion may be inferred. He divides the pairings into three groups or 'figures', and his discussion proceeds in a rigorous and orderly fashion. The pairings are taken according to a fixed pattern, and for each pair Aristotle states, and proves formally, what conclusion, if any, may be inferred. The whole account is recognized as the first essay in the science of formal logic.

The logical theory of the *Prior Analytics* is known as 'Aristotle's syllogistic'. The Greek word '*sullogismos*' is explained by Aristotle as follows: 'A *sullogismos* is an argument in which, certain things being assumed, something different from the things assumed follows from necessity by the fact that they hold'. The theory of the *Prior Analytics* is a theory of the *sullogismos* — a theory, as we might put it, of deductive inference.

Aristotle makes great claims for his theory: 'every proof and every deductive inference (*sullogismos*) must come about through the three figures that we have described'; in other words, every possible deductive inference can be shown to consist of a sequence of one or more arguments of the type which Aristotle has analysed. Aristotle is, in effect, claiming that he has produced a complete and perfect logic; and he offers a complex argument in favour of the claim. The argument is defective, and the claim is false. Moreover, the theory inherits the weaknesses of the account of propositions on which it is based – and it contains a number of internal deficiencies to boot. None the less, later thinkers were so impressed by the power of Aristotle's exposition that for more than a thousand years Aristotelian syllogistic was taught as though it contained the sum of logical truth. And indeed on any account, the *Prior Analytics* – the very first attempt to develop a science of logic – is a work of outstanding genius. It is elegant and systematic; its arguments are orderly, lucid, and rigorous; and it achieves a remarkable level of generality.

Chapter 8
Knowledge

The logic of the *Prior Analytics* serves to derive the theorems of a science from its axioms. The *Posterior Analytics* is primarily concerned to study the nature of the axioms themselves, and hence the general form of an axiomatized deductive science. To a surprising extent, the *Posterior Analytics* is independent of the syllogistical theory developed in the *Prior Analytics*: whatever the explanation for this fact may be, it has a happy consequence – the deficiencies in Aristotle's theory of inference are not all inherited by his theory of axiomatization.

Aristotle's account of the nature of axioms is based upon his conception of the nature of knowledge; for a science is meant to systematize our knowledge of its subject-matter, and its component axioms and theorems must therefore be propositions which are known and which satisfy the conditions set upon knowledge. According to Aristotle, 'we think we know a thing (in the unqualified sense, and not in the sophistical sense or accidentally) when we think we know both the cause because of which the thing is (and know that it is its cause) and also that it is not possible for it to be otherwise'. A zoologist, then, will know that cows have four stomachs if, first, he knows why they do (if he knows that they have four stomachs because of such-and-such a fact) and, secondly, he knows that cows must have four stomachs (that it does not merely happen to be the case that they do). Those two conditions set upon knowledge govern Aristotle's whole approach to axiomatic science in the *Posterior Analytics*.

The first condition set upon knowledge is a condition of causality. The word 'cause' must be taken in a broad sense: it translates the Greek '*aitia*', which some scholars prefer to render by 'explanation'. To cite a 'cause' of something is to explain why it is so.

The condition of causality is linked to a number of other requirements which the axioms of any science must satisfy.

> If knowing is what we have laid it down to be, demonstrative knowledge must be based upon things which are true and primary and immediate, and more known than and prior to and causes of the conclusion; for thus the principles will be appropriate to what is being proved. There can be an inference without these conditions, but there cannot be a proof; for it will not yield knowledge.

Aristotle

The principles or starting-points of demonstrative knowledge are the axioms on which the science is based; and Aristotle's general point is that those principles or axioms must satisfy certain requirements if the system they ground is to be a science, a system of knowledge.

Clearly, the axioms must be true. Otherwise they could neither be known themselves nor ground our knowledge of the theorems. Equally clearly, they must be 'immediate and primary'. Otherwise there will be truths prior to them from which they can be derived – and thus they will not after all be axioms or first principles. Again, in so far as our knowledge of the theorems depends upon the axioms, it is reasonable to say that the axioms must be 'more known' than the theorems.

It is the final condition in Aristotle's list, that the axioms be 'prior to and causes of the conclusion', which is linked most directly to his account of what knowledge is. Our knowledge of the theorems rests upon the axioms, and knowledge involves a grasp of causes: hence the axioms must state the ultimate causes which account for the facts expressed by the theorems. A man who reads through an axiomatized science, starting from the axioms and proceeding through the successive theorems, will in effect be reading off a list of causally connected facts.

At first glance, the causality condition seems odd. Why should we suppose that knowing something requires knowing its cause? Surely we know large numbers of facts about whose causes we are quite in the dark? (We know that inflation occurs; but economists cannot tell us why it does. We know that the Second World War broke out in 1939; but historians dispute among themselves about the causes of the war.) Moreover, the causality condition appears to threaten an infinite regress. Suppose I know X; then according to Aristotle I must know the cause of X. Call that Y. Then it seems to follow that I must know the cause of Y too; and so on *ad infinitum*.

The second of those problems was explicitly discussed by Aristotle. He held that there are some facts which are causally primary, or which have no causes apart from themselves; and he sometimes expresses this by saying that they are self-caused or self-explanatory. Why do cows have horns? Because they are deficient in teeth (so that the matter which would have formed teeth goes to make horns). Why are they deficient in teeth? Because they have four stomachs (and so can digest their food unchewed). Why do they have four stomachs? Because they are ruminants. Why, then, are cows ruminants? Simply because they are cows – there is no further feature, apart from their being cows, which explains why cows are ruminants; the cause of a cow's being a ruminant is just its being a cow.

That cows are ruminants is self-explanatory. Aristotle usually says that such self-explanatory facts are definitions, or parts of definitions; so that the axioms of the sciences will for the most part consist of definitions. A definition, in Aristotle's sense, is not a statement of what some word means. (It is no part of the meaning of the word 'cow' that cows are ruminants; for we all know what 'cow' means long before we know that cows are ruminants.) Rather, definitions state the essence of a thing, what it is to be that thing. (It is part of the essential nature of a cow that it is a ruminant; what it is to be a cow is to be a ruminant animal of a certain kind.) Some modern philosophers have rejected – and ridiculed – Aristotle's talk of essences. But Aristotle shows himself the better scientist; for an important part of the scientific endeavour consists in explaining the various quirks and properties of substances and stuffs in terms of their fundamental natures – that is to say, in terms of their essences. Aristotle's axiomatic sciences will start from essences and successively explain derivative properties. The theorems of animal biology, say, will express the derived properties of animals, and the deduction of the theorems from the axioms will show how those properties are dependent upon the relevant essences.

But must all knowledge be causal or explanatory in this way? Although Aristotle's official view is that 'we know each thing only when we know its cause', he often uses the word 'know' – just as we do – in cases where the cause escapes us. And Aristotle is surely mistaken in asserting that knowledge is always causal. But it would be short-sighted simply to lament the mistake and pass on. Aristotle, like Plato before him, was primarily concerned with a special type of knowledge – with what we may call scientific understanding; and it is plausible to claim that scientific understanding involves knowledge of causes. Although we may know quite well that inflation occurs without being able to say why it does, we cannot claim to understand the phenomenon of inflation until we have a grasp of its causes, and the science of economics is imperfect until it can supply such a causal understanding. Taken as a piece of lexicography, Aristotle's definition of 'knowledge' is false; construed as a remark about the nature of the scientific enterprise, it expresses an important truth.

So much for the condition of causality. The second condition in Aristotle's account of knowledge is that what is known must be the case of necessity: if you know something, that thing cannot be otherwise. In the *Posterior Analytics* Aristotle elaborates the point. He connects it with the thesis that only universal propositions can be known. He infers that 'the conclusion of such a proof must be eternal – therefore there is no proof or knowledge about things which can be destroyed'.

The necessity condition with its two corollaries seems no less strange than the causality condition. Surely we do have knowledge of contingent facts (for example, that the population of the world is increasing), and of particular facts (for example, that Aristotle was born in 384 BC). Moreover, many of the sciences seem to countenance such knowledge. Astronomy, for example, deals with particular objects – with the sun and the moon and the stars, and the case is similar with geography, which Aristotle studied in his *Meteorology*, and, most obviously, with history. Aristotle, it is true, thinks that the objects of astronomy are not perishable but eternal. He also holds that 'poetry is more philosophical and more serious than history – for poetry tends to describe what is universal, history what is particular'. (History, in other words, is not granted full scientific status.) But that does not alter the fact that some sciences deal unequivocally with particulars.

Furthermore, Aristotle believed (as we shall shortly see) that the basic entities of the world are perishable particulars, and it would be paradoxical if he were driven to the view that there is no scientific knowledge of these fundamental objects. In any case, Aristotle is wrong to infer from the necessity condition that knowledge must be about eternal objects. It is a universal and perhaps a necessary truth that the parents of a human being are human ('a man', as Aristotle puts it, 'generates a man'). You might perhaps say it is an eternal truth – at least, it is always true. But it is not a truth about eternal objects: it is a truth about mortal, perishable men. Moreover,

Aristotle himself concludes, at the end of a tangled argument, that 'to say that all knowledge is universal . . . is in a way true and in a way not true . . . It is clear that knowledge is in a way universal and in a way not.' Thus he allows that there is, 'in a way', knowledge of particulars; and we must dismiss the second corollary of the necessity condition as a mistake.

As for the first corollary, I have already remarked that in Aristotle's opinion the theorems of science do not always hold universally and of necessity: some of them hold only 'for the most part', and what holds 'for the most part' is explicitly distinguished from what holds always. 'All knowledge deals either with what holds always or with what holds for the most part (how else could one either learn it or teach it to someone else?); for it must be determined either by what holds always or by what holds for the most part – for example, that honeywater for the most part benefits the feverish.' Aristotle's assertion that scientific propositions must be universal is an exaggeration, on his own admission; and the same must be said for the necessity condition itself.

Science strives for generality; in order to understand particular occurrences we must see them as part of some general pattern. Aristotle's view that knowledge is of what cannot be otherwise is a reflection of that important fact. But it is a distorted reflection, and the necessity condition laid down in the *Posterior Analytics* is too stringent.

Chapter 9
Ideal and Achievement

Aristotle has emerged as a systematic thinker. The various sciences are autonomous but systematically interrelated. Each individual science is to be developed and presented in the form of an axiomatic system – 'in the geometrical manner', as later philosophers put it. Moreover, the set of concepts within which Aristotle's notion of science finds its place was itself systematically examined and ordered. Perhaps none of that is surprising. Philosophy, after all, is nothing if not systematic, and Aristotle's system – his 'world picture' – has for centuries been held up for admiration and praise.

Some scholars, however, have disputed this view of Aristotle. They have denied that he was a system-builder. Themselves distrusting the grandiose claims of systematic philosophy, they find Aristotle's virtues to lie elsewhere. For them, Aristotle's philosophy is essentially 'aporetic': it consists in the posing of particular puzzles or *aporiai*, and in the development of particular solutions to them. Aristotle's thought is tentative, flexible, changing. He does not sketch a grand design and then fill in the details; nor does he follow a single method towards a single goal. Rather, the details are all; and the methods and modes of argument vary with the topics to which they are addressed. Aristotle works piecemeal.

This anti-systematic interpretation of Aristotle's thought is now widely accepted. It has much to be said in its favour. Book III of the *Metaphysics*, for example, consists of a long catalogue of puzzles, and much of the remainder of the *Metaphysics* is given over to their solution. Or consider the following passage: 'here, as elsewhere, we must set down the phenomena and first go through the puzzles; then we must prove the reputable opinions about these matters – if possible, all of them, if not, the majority and the most important'. First, set down prevailing views on the matter ('the phenomena', or 'the things which seem to be the case', are the reputable opinions on the subject); then go through the puzzles which those views raise (because they are obscure, perhaps, or because they are mutually inconsistent); finally, prove all or most of the views to be true. That is no recipe for system-building; yet it is a recipe which Aristotle commends and which he sometimes follows.

Moreover, the aporetic interpretation seems to do justice to an aspect of Aristotle's work which on the traditional interpretation must perplex. Aristotle's scientific treatises are never presented in an axiomatic fashion. The prescriptions of the *Posterior Analytics* are not followed in, say, the *Meteorology* or the *Parts of Animals*. Those treatises do not lay down axioms and then proceed to deduce theorems; rather, they present, and attempt to answer, a connected sequence of problems. On the traditional view, the treatises must seem – to put it paradoxically – wholly un-Aristotelian: the trumpeted system is simply not apparent in their pages. On the aporetic interpretation, the treatises represent the essence of Aristotle's philosophy: his occasional reflections on systematization are not to be taken too seriously – they are ritual gestures towards a Platonic notion of science, not evidence of Aristotle's own fundamental convictions.

It is undeniable that many of Aristotle's treatises are, in large part, aporetic in style – that they discuss problems, and discuss them piecemeal. It is also undeniable that the treatises contain little or nothing in the way of axiomatized development. But it does not follow

10. The site of the Lyceum, unearthed in 1996. 'The Lyceum was not a private college: it was a public place – a sanctuary and a gymnasium. An old story tells that Aristotle lectured to his chosen pupils in the mornings and to the general public in the evenings.'

that Aristotle was not at bottom a systematic thinker; and the theory of science expounded in the *Posterior Analytics* cannot be dismissed as an irrelevant archaism, a genuflection to Plato's ghost. There are so many hints and intimations of systematization in the treatises that the solution of *aporiai* cannot be regarded as the be-all and end-all of Aristotle's scientific and philosophical enquiries; and – a point worth underlining – even the piecemeal discussions of individual problems are given an intellectual unity by the common conceptual framework within which they are examined and answered. Systematization is not achieved in the treatises; but it is an ideal, ever present in the background.

What, then, are we to say of the unsystematic features of Aristotle's works? First, not all of Aristotle's treatises are works of science: many are works about science. The *Posterior Analytics* is a case in point. That treatise is not presented axiomatically; but then it is a treatise about the axiomatic method – it is concerned not to develop a science but rather to examine the way in which a science should be developed. Again, many parts of the *Physics* and of the *Metaphysics* are essays on what we might call the foundations of science. We should not expect that writings about the structure and grounds of science will themselves exhibit the features which they demand of writings within the sciences.

But what of the aporetic aspects of Aristotle's properly scientific works? Why are the *Meteorology* and the *Parts of Animals*, say, not presented axiomatically? The answer is simple. Aristotle's system is a design for finished or completed sciences. The *Posterior Analytics* does not describe the activities of the scientific researcher: it determines the form in which the researcher's results are to be systematically organized and displayed. The sciences which Aristotle knew and to which he contributed were not complete, nor did he take them to be. Perhaps he had his optimistic moments: Cicero reports that 'Aristotle, accusing the old philosophers who thought that philosophy had been perfected by their own efforts, says that they were either very stupid or very vain; but that he himself could see that, since great advances had been made in so few years, philosophy would be completely finished in a short time.' But in fact Aristotle never boasts of having completed any branch of knowledge – save perhaps the science of logic.

Aristotle says enough to enable us to see how, in a perfect world, he would have presented and organized the scientific knowledge which he had industriously amassed. But his systematic plans are plans for a completed science, and he himself did not live long enough to discover everything. Since the treatises are not the final presentations of an achieved science, we should not expect to find in them an orderly succession of axioms and deductions. Since the treatises are intended, in the end, to convey a systematic science, we should expect them to indicate how that system is to be achieved. And that is exactly what we do find: Aristotle was a systematic thinker; his surviving treatises present a partial and unfinished sketch of his system.

Chapter 10
Reality

Science is about real things. That is what makes it knowledge rather than fantasy. But what things are real? What are the fundamental items with which science must concern itself? That is the question of ontology, and a question to which Aristotle devoted much attention. One of his ontological essays, the *Categories*, is relatively clear; but most of his ontological thought is to be found in the *Metaphysics*, and in some of the most obscure parts of that obscure work.

'Now the question which, both now and in the past, is continually posed and continually puzzled over is this: What is being? That is, what is substance?' Before sketching Aristotle's answer to that question we must ask about the question itself. What is Aristotle after? What does he mean by 'substance'? This preliminary question is best approached by a circuitous route.

The *Categories* is concerned with classifying types of predicate ('*katêgoria*' is Aristotle's word for 'predicate'). Consider a particular subject, say Aristotle himself. We can ask various types of question about him: *What* is he? – He is a man, an animal, etc. What are his *qualities*? – He is pale, intelligent, etc. How large is he? – He is five feet ten and ten stone eight. How is he *related* to other things? – He is Nicomachus' son, Pythias' husband. *Where* is he? – He is in the Lyceum. . . . Different types of question are answered appropriately

ΑΡΙΣΤΟΤΕΛΟΥΣ ΤΑ ΜΕΤΑ ΤΑ ΦΥΣΙΚΑ

ARISTOTLE'S
METAPHYSICS

A REVISED TEXT
WITH INTRODUCTION AND COMMENTARY

BY

W. D. ROSS

FELLOW OF ORIEL COLLEGE
DEPUTY PROFESSOR OF MORAL PHILOSOPHY IN THE
UNIVERSITY OF OXFORD

VOLUME I

OXFORD
AT THE CLARENDON PRESS
1924

11. 'All men by nature desire to know': the optimistic opening of Aristotle's *Metaphysics*. The title-page of Sir David Ross's edition of the *Metaphysics*, first published at Oxford in 1924.

by different types of predicate. The question 'How large?' attracts predicates of *quantity*, the question 'How related?' attracts predicates of *relation*, and so on. Aristotle thinks that there are ten such classes of predicate; and he offers to characterize each class. For example, 'what is really peculiar to quantities is that they can be called equal and unequal'; or 'in respect of qualities alone are things called like and unlike'. Not all of Aristotle's classes are equally clearly delineated, and his discussion of what belongs to what class contains some puzzles. Again it is not clear why Aristotle settles for *ten* classes. (He rarely makes use, outside the *Categories*, of all ten classes; and he was probably not firmly committed to that precise number.) But the general point is plain enough: predicates fall into different classes.

Aristotle's classes of predicates are themselves now called 'categories', the term 'category' having been transferred from the things classified to the things into which they are classified, so that it is normal to talk of 'Aristotle's ten categories'. More importantly, the categories are generally referred to as categories 'of being' – and indeed Aristotle himself will sometimes refer to them as 'the classes of the things that exist'. Why the switch from classes of predicates to classes of beings? Suppose that the predicate 'healthy' is true of Aristotle: then health is one of Aristotle's qualities, and there must *be* such a thing as health. In general, if any predicate is true of anything, then that thing has a certain property – the property corresponding to the predicate. And the things or properties corresponding to predicates may themselves be classified in a way corresponding to the classification of the predicates. Or rather, there is only one classification: in classifying predicates, we thereby classify properties; in saying that the predicate applied to Aristotle in the sentence 'Aristotle is healthy' is a predicate of quality, or that the predicate applied to him in 'Aristotle is in the Lyceum' is a predicate of place, we are saying that health is a quality, or that the Lyceum is a place. Things, like predicates, come in different sorts; and if there are ten classes or categories of predicate, there are ten classes or categories of things.

Predicates which answer the question 'What is so-and-so?' fall into the category which Aristotle calls 'substance', and the things which belong to the category are substances. The class of substances is peculiarly important; for it is primary. In order to understand the primacy of substance we must turn briefly to a notion of central significance to Aristotle's whole thought.

Aristotle noticed that certain Greek terms are ambiguous. 'Sharp', for example, in Greek as in English, can be applied to sounds as well as to knives; and it is plain that it is one thing for a sound to be sharp and quite another for a knife to be sharp. Many ambiguities are easily detected: they may provide puns, but they do not provide puzzlement. But ambiguity is sometimes more subtle, and it sometimes infects terms of philosophical importance. Aristotle thought that most of the key terms in philosophy were ambiguous. In the *Sophistical Refutations* he spends some time in expounding and solving sophistical puzzles that are based on ambiguity, and Book V of the *Metaphysics*, sometimes called Aristotle's 'philosophical lexicon', is a set of short essays on the different senses of a number of philosophical terms. 'Something is called a cause in one way if . . ., in another if.. . .'; 'Something is said to be necessary if . . ., or if . . .'. And so on, for many of the terms central to Aristotle's own philosophical system.

One of the terms which Aristotle recognizes as ambiguous is the term 'being' or 'existent'. Chapter 7 of Book V of the *Metaphysics* is given over to 'being'; and Book VII begins by observing that 'things are said to be in many senses, as we described earlier in our remarks on ambiguity; for being signifies what a thing is (that is, this so-and-so), and quality or quantity or each of the other things predicated in this way'. There are at least as many senses of 'being', then, as there are categories of beings.

Some ambiguities are merely 'chance homonymies' – as with the Greek word '*kleis*' which means both 'bolt' and 'collar-bone'. Aristotle does not mean that it was a matter of chance that '*kleis*' was applied to collar-bones as well as to bolts (that would be evidently false, and many ambiguities have some sort of rough similarity to explain their existence). What he means is that there is no connection of meaning between the two uses of the term: you could be perfectly capable of using the word in one of its senses without having an inkling of the other. But not all ambiguities are 'chance homonymies' in this sense, and in particular the word 'be' or 'exist' does not present a chance homonymy: 'things are said to exist in many ways, but with reference to one thing and to some single nature, and not homonymously' ('not homonymously' here means 'not by chance homonymy'). Aristotle illustrates what he has in mind by two non-philosophical examples:

> Everything that is healthy is so called with reference to health – some things by preserving it, some by producing it, some by being signs of health, some because they are receptive of it; and things are called medical with reference to the art of medicine – for some things are called medical by possessing the art of medicine, others by being well adapted to it, others by being instruments of the art of medicine. And we shall find other things called in a similar manner to these.

The term 'healthy' is ambiguous. We call all sorts of things – men, spas, foodstuffs – healthy; but George V, Bognor Regis, and All Bran are not all healthy in the same sense. Yet the different senses of 'healthy' are interconnected, and their interconnection is determined by the fact that all refer to some one thing, namely health. Thus for George V to be healthy is for him to *possess* health; for Bognor Regis to be healthy is for it to *produce* health; for All Bran to be healthy is for it to *preserve* health; and so on. 'Some single nature' enters into the explanation of what it is for each of these diverse things to be diversely healthy.

So too with the term 'medical', which in a similar way focuses on the science of medicine. So too, according to Aristotle, with 'being' or 'existence'.

> Thus things are said in many ways to exist, but all with reference to one starting-point. For some are said to exist because they are substances, others because they are affections of substances, others because they are paths to substance or destructions or privations or qualities or producers or creators of substances or of things said to exist by reference to substance, or are negations of these or of substance.

Just as everything called healthy is so called with reference to health, so everything said to be or to exist is so said with reference to substance. There exist colours and sizes, changes and destructions, places and times. But for a colour to exist is for some *substance* to be coloured, for a size to exist is for some *substance* to have it, for a movement to exist is for some *substance* to move. Non-substances exist, but they are parasites – they exist only as modifications or affections of substances. For a non-substance to exist is for an existing substance to be modified in some way or other. But the existence of substances is not parasitic: substances exist in a primary sense; for a substance to exist is *not* for something else – something non-substantial – to be as it were, substantified.

The term 'exist', like the term 'healthy', possesses unity in diversity; and 'exist' focuses on substance just as 'healthy' focuses on health. That is the chief way in which the class of substances is primary in relation to the other categories of being.

Then what is it to be a substance? Substance predicates are predicates which provide decent answers to the question 'What is it?'. Men are substances; that is to say, 'man' is a substance-predicate – for 'He is a man' is a decent answer to the question 'What is Aristotle?'. But the 'What is it?' question is far too imprecise. In Book V of the *Metaphysics* Aristotle supplements, or supplants, it by a different criterion for being a substance: 'things are called substances in two ways: whatever is the ultimate subject, which is no longer said of anything else; and whatever, being this so-and-so, is also separable'. The second way in which things are called substances couples two notions frequently employed by Aristotle in his reflections on the question: a substance is 'this so-and-so', and it is also 'separable'.

'This so-and-so' translates the Greek '*tode ti*', an odd sort of phrase which Aristotle nowhere explains. What he seems to have in mind can perhaps be expressed in the following way. Substances are things to which we can refer by use of a demonstrative phrase of the form '*this* so-and-so'; they are things that can be picked out, identified, individuated. Socrates, for instance, is an example of a 'this so-and-so'; for he is *this man* – an individual whom we can pick out and identify.

But what about, say, Socrates' complexion, his paleness? Can we not refer to that by the phrase 'this paleness'? Is this paleness not something which we can identify and reidentify? Aristotle says that 'the particular pale is in a subject, namely the body (for all colour is in a body)', and by 'the particular pale' he appears to mean 'this paleness', an individual instance of the quality of being pale. But even if this paleness is an individual thing, it does not follow that we must allow it to be a substance. For a substance is not only 'this so-and-so': it is also 'separable'. What is separability here?

It seems that Socrates might exist without his paleness but that Socrates' paleness cannot exist without Socrates. Socrates may lie on the beach and so cease to be pallid: he is there without his pallor – but his pallor cannot be there without him. Socrates is separable from his paleness. Socrates' paleness is not separable from Socrates. That is perhaps part of what Aristotle means by separability; but it is probably not a complete account. For one thing, Socrates may cease to be pale, but he cannot cease to be coloured; he may be separable from paleness, but he is not in the same way separable from colour.

We need to refer again to Aristotle's account of the ambiguity of being. Some things, we saw, are parasitic upon others: a parasitic item exists insofar as some other existent to be somehow related to it. There is a connection between parasitism and separation: a thing is separable if it is not parasitic. Socrates is separable from his paleness, because for Socrates to exist is not for his paleness to be modified in a certain way; Socrates' paleness is not separable from Socrates, because for it to exist is for some other thing, namely Socrates, to be pale. Socrates is separable from his paleness. He is also separable from his colour; for although he must have some colour or other, his existence is not a matter of colour being modified in some way or other. In general, Socrates is separable from everything else: for Socrates to exist is not a matter of something else being thus and so.

Then what is a substance? A thing is a substance if, and only if, it is both an individual (a 'this so-and-so', something capable of being designated by a demonstrative phrase), and also a separable item (something non-parasitic, a thing whose existence is not a matter of some other thing's being modified in some way or other).

We can now return to Aristotle's eternal question: What things in fact are substances? We should not expect a simple and authoritative answer from Aristotle (after all, he says that the question is perpetually puzzling), and in fact his attempted answers are hesitant and difficult to understand. But one or two things emerge fairly clearly. Aristotle's predecessors had, he thought, implicitly offered a number of different answers to the question. Some had held that stuffs – gold, flesh, earth, water – were substances (he is thinking primarily of the earliest Greek philosophers, who focused their attention on the material constituents of things). Others had held that the ultimate parts of ordinary things were substances (Aristotle is thinking of the ancient atomists, whose basic entities were microscopical corpuscles). Yet other thinkers had proposed that numbers were substances (the Pythagoreans and certain of Plato's followers fall into this camp). Finally, some had decided that substances are only to be found among certain abstract entities or universals (Plato's doctrine of Forms is the outstanding example of such a theory). Chalk, a gaggle of quarks, the prime numbers, Truth and Beauty – all are, or were held to be, prime candidates for substancehood.

Aristotle rejected all the candidates. 'It is plain that of the things that are thought to be substances, most are powers – both the parts of animals . . . and earth and fire and air.' For earth to exist, we might say, is for certain substances to have certain powers (in Aristotle's view, for them to have the power or tendency to move downwards); and for fire to exist is for certain substances to heat and burn and to have a tendency to rise. As for the parts of animals, 'all these are defined by their functions; for each is truly such if it can perform its own function – for example, an eye, if it can see – and what cannot do so is an eye only homonymously (for example, a dead one or one made of stone)'. An eye is something that can see; for eyes to exist is for animals to be capable of seeing.

So much for stuffs and for parts. As for numbers, they are plainly non-substantial. The number three exists just in so far as there are groups of three things. Numbers are essentially numbers of things, and although the number ten is not identical with any or every group of ten items, still the existence of the number ten consists precisely in there being such groups or sets of ten substances. Such at least is the view which Aristotle develops in the last two books of the *Metaphysics*.

He devotes most of his polemical attention to the fourth candidate for substancehood. Plato's theory of Forms was by far the most elaborate ontological theory with which Aristotle was acquainted, and it was a theory to which, in his years in the Academy, he was perpetually exposed. Aristotle's arguments against the Platonic theory were first set out in a special treatise *On the Ideas*, which survives only in fragments. He returned to the attack again and again, and produced a battery of considerations against the theory. Many of these arguments concern detailed aspects of Plato's view; but some of them are wholly

12. Fragment of a dialogue on Platonic metaphysics, perhaps from Aristotle's lost work *On Ideas*. The text is in mirror-writing on a lump of mud: the mud absorbed the ink from a piece of papyrus and the papyrus rotted away. The fragment was found in Afghanistan – see illustration on page 138.

general, and they apply with equal force to any theory which takes universal items such as Truth and Beauty to be substances.

Aristotle held that whiteness exists insofar as certain substances are white. Plato, on the contrary, held that a substance is white insofar as it shares in whiteness. In Aristotle's opinion, white things are prior to whiteness, for the existence of whiteness is simply a matter of there being white things. In Plato's opinion, whiteness is prior to white things, for the existence of white things is simply a matter of their sharing in whiteness. Aristotle's arguments against this Platonic notion are powerful; but they have not convinced determined Platonists – nor is it easy to see how the dispute might be settled.

If Platonism goes the way of the other three accounts of substance, then what is to be said? What are Aristotelian substances? The answer is robust and commonsensical. The first and plainest examples of substances are animals and plants; to these we may add other natural bodies (the sun, the moon, and the stars, for example), and perhaps also artefacts (tables and chairs, pots and pans). In general, perceptible things – middle-sized material objects – are the primary furniture of Aristotle's world; and it is significant that he often poses his ontological question by asking if there are any substances apart from perceptible substances. Such, in Aristotle's view, are the basic realities, and the things with which science principally concerns itself.

Chapter 11
Change

Can we say anything more, in general terms, about those middle-sized material objects which are the chief substances in Aristotle's world? One of their most important features is that they change. Unlike Plato's Forms, which exist eternally and are always the same, Aristotle's substances are for the most part temporary items which undergo a variety of alterations. There are, in Aristotle's view, four types of change: a thing can change in respect of substance, of quality, of quantity, and of place. Change in respect of substance is coming-into-being and going-out-of-existence, or generation and destruction: such changes occurs when a cat is born and when it dies, when a statue is made and when it is smashed. Change in respect of quality is called alteration: a plant alters when it grows green in the sunlight or pale in the dark; a wax candle alters when it grows soft in the heat or hardens in the cold. Change in respect of quantity is growth and diminution; and natural objects typically begin by growing and end by diminishing. Finally, change in respect of place is motion. Most of the *Physics* is devoted to a study of change in its different forms. For the *Physics* studies the philosophical background to natural science; and 'nature is a principle of motion and change', so that 'things have a nature if they possess such a principle'. That is to say, the very subject-matter of natural science consists of moving and changing things.

Aristotle's predecessors had been puzzled by the phenomena of

PHYSICORVM

ARISTOTELIS

LIBRI,

IOACHIMO PERIONIO
interprete:nunc verò opera doĉtif-
simi Nicolai Grouchij inte-
grè reftituti,limati,
& emendati.

QVORVM SERIEM
pagina fequens in-
dicabit.

IN VIRTVTE, ET FORTVNA.

LVGDVNI,
APVD GVLIEL. ROVILLIVM,
SVB SCVTO VENETO.
M. D. LXI.

13. Title-page of an edition of the *Physics* published at Lyons in 1561. 'Most of the *Physics* is devoted to a study of change in its different forms. For the *Physics* studies the philosopical background to natural science; and "nature is a principle of motion and change".'

change: Heraclitus had thought that change was perpetual and essential to the real world; Parmenides had denied the very possibility of coming-into-being, and hence of any sort of change; Plato had argued that the ordinary changing world could not be a subject of scientific knowledge. In the first books of the *Physics* Aristotle argues that every change involves three things. There is the state from which the change proceeds, the state to which the change proceeds, and the object which persists through the change. In Book V the account is embellished slightly: 'there is something which initiates the change, and something which is changing, and again something in which the change takes place (the time); and apart from these, something from which and something to which. For all change is from something to something; for the thing changing is different from that to which it is changing and from that from which – for example, the log, the hot, the cold'. When a log becomes hot in the grate, it changes from a state of coldness; it changes to a state of hotness; the log itself persists through the change; the change takes some time; and there was something – perhaps my lighting the match – which initiated the change.

That in every change there is an initial state and an end state is surely obvious; and the states must be distinct, or else no change will have occurred. (An object may change from white to black, and then back to white again. But if its colour is the same throughout a given period, then it has not changed colour during that period.) Again, in the case of qualitative change, of quantitative change, and of locomotion, it is plain that there must be an item which persists through the change. On the one hand, 'there is no change apart from the things that change', or 'all change is a change of something'; on the other hand, this 'something' must persist (for it is one thing for my full glass to become empty, another for it to be replaced by an empty glass). So far so good; but Aristotle's analysis appears to have some difficulty with change in substance.

It is easy to imagine that the two end-states in generation and destruction are non-existence and existence. When Socrates came into being, he changed from a state of non-existence to a state of existence; and when he died he made the reverse change. But a moment's reflection shows the absurdity of this idea. For Socrates does not persist through his generation, nor does he persist through his destruction. On the contrary, these two changes mark the beginning and the ending of Socrates' existence. At this point Aristotle observes that substances – material bodies – are in a sense composite. A house, for example, consists of bricks and timbers arranged in a certain structure; a statue consists of marble or bronze carved or cast into a certain shape; an animal consists of tissues (flesh, blood, and the rest) organized on certain principles. All substances thus consist of two 'parts', stuff and structure, which Aristotle habitually calls 'matter' and 'form'. Matter and form are not physical parts of substances; nor can you cut up a bronze statue into two separate bits, its bronze and its shape. On the other hand, we must not imagine the matter as the physical aspect of a substance and the form as some sort of non-physical additive: the shape of a football is just as physical an aspect as its leathery texture. Rather, matter and form are logical parts of substances; that is to say, an account of what some specific substance is – an account of what a statue is or of what an octopus is – will require mention both of its stuff and of its structure.

We can now see that 'whatever comes into being must always be divisible, and be part thus and part thus – I mean part matter and part form'. And

> it becomes clear ... that substances ... come into being from some underlying subject; for there must always be something that underlies, from which what comes into being comes into being – for example, plants and animals from seed. And the things that come into being do so in some cases by change of shape (for example, statues), in some by addition (for example, growing things), in some by subtraction (for

example, a marble Hermes), in some by putting together (for example, a house) . . .

When a statue comes into being or is made, the persisting object is not the statue itself but the matter of the statue, the mass of bronze or the block of marble. The end-states are not non-existence and existence, but shapelessness and shapeliness. When a man comes into being, what persists is the stuff, not the man; and the stuff is first non-human and then human.

This account of the nature of change had the merit of allowing Aristotle to overcome many of the difficulties about change which his predecessors had raised. But it is not wholly compelling. Thomas Aquinas, one of Aristotle's most sympathetic critics, observed that the theory rules out the possibility of creation. Aquinas's God had created the world out of nothing. The world once came into being, and that was, in Aristotle's terms, a substantial change. But the change was not the imposition of a new form on a mass of pre-existing matter: there was no pre-existing matter; and when God created the world he produced the stuff at the same time as he devised the structure. If you reflect solely on the sublunary world, Aquinas says, you may be inclined to accept Aristotle's analysis of change. But if you look higher you will see that not all change will fit the analysis. Whether or not we agree with Aquinas's theology, we may accept the core of his criticism; for we surely cannot rule out creation on purely logical grounds. But if Aristotle's account of change is too restrictive, that is of no great moment for his theory of science; for that theory is primarily concerned with ordinary, sublunary, changing things.

Strictly speaking, what I have described so far is not Aristotle's account of change itself, but rather his account of the pre-conditions for change. At any rate, in Book III of the *Physics* he poses the question 'What is change?', and gives an answer which is meant to complement the discussion of the first book. His answer is this: 'Change is the actuality of the potential *qua* such.' (That sentence is often cited as Aristotle's definition of motion. The word 'motion' in English usually means 'change of place', 'locomotion'. Aristotle's word here is '*kinêsis*': though the term is sometimes restricted to locomotion, it usually means 'change' in general, and in Book III of the *Physics* it has its usual meaning.) Aristotle's critics have pounced upon this sentence as an example of pompous obscurantism. It deserves a brief commentary.

The terms 'actuality' and 'potentiality' form a refrain in Aristotle's treatises. They serve to mark the difference between something which is actually so-and-so and something which is potentially so-and-so; between, say, a builder who is slapping mortar on bricks, and a builder on holiday (a builder who is not building but retains the pertinent skills and capacities). It is one thing to have a capacity, another to exercise it; one thing to possess potential, another to actualize it. Aristotle makes a number of claims about the distinction between actuality and potentiality, some of them acute, some dubious. He holds, for example, that 'actuality is in all cases prior to potentiality both in definition and in substance; and in time it is in a way prior and in a way not'. The first point is true; for in order to define a potentiality we must specify what it is a potentiality for, and in so doing we name an actuality. (To be a builder is to be capable of building, to be visible is to be able to be seen.) Since the reverse is not true (actuality does not in the same way presuppose potentiality), an actuality is prior in definition to its correlative potentiality. On the other hand, the claim that actuality is prior to potentiality in time is less persuasive. Aristotle means that before there can be any potential so-and-sos, there must be actual so-and-sos – before there can be any potential men (that is any stuff that may become human), there must be actual men. For, he says, 'in all cases what is actually so-and-so comes into being from what is potentially so-and-so by the agency of something actually so-and-so – for example, men from men, a musical person by the agency of a musical person. There is always something which initiates the change, and what initiates the change is itself actually so-and-so'. In general, any change requires a cause; and in general, you cause something to be so-and-so inasmuch as you transmit a certain character to it, and you can only transmit what you yourself possess. Thus if someone comes to be musical he must have been caused to be musical by someone or something; the causal agent, since it transmitted musicality, must itself have been actually musical. Hence the actually musical must be there in order for the potentially musical to realize its potential. Aristotle's argument is ingenious; but it is not conclusive. First, it cannot show that the actual is prior to the potential but only that the actual is prior to the actualization of the potential. Secondly, it relies on shaky principles of causation – for example, causation need not be, and usually is not, a matter of transmission.

'Change is the actuality of the potential *qua* such.' Actuality and potentiality for what? The answer emerges in the course of Aristotle's argument: it is the potentiality to be changing. In place of Aristotle's obscure sentence we may therefore write: 'Change is the actuality of the changeable *qua* changeable.' Now this is supposed to explain what it is for something to be changing. Then let us replace Aristotle's abstract nouns 'change' and 'actuality' by modest verbs: 'Something is in the process of changing whenever it possesses a capacity to change and is exercising that capacity.' This paraphrase surely reduces the obscurity of Aristotle's analysis, but it appears to do so at a price – the price of banality. For the analysis becomes a tautology.

Or perhaps not. Perhaps Aristotle did not intend to offer an illuminating definition of change but rather to make a particular point about the sort of actuality involved in change. Aristotle thinks that some actualities are incompatible with their correlative potentialities. What is white cannot become white. What is actually white is not at the same time potentially white. Before being painted white, the ceiling was potentially but not actually white; now, after being painted, it is actually but no longer potentially white. Other actualities are different: being actually so-and-so is quite compatible with still being potentially so-and-so. When I am actually smoking a pipe, I am still capable of smoking a pipe (otherwise I could not puff on). When a steeplechaser is actually galloping over the course, he is still capable of galloping (otherwise he would never reach the finishing-post). The point of Aristotle's 'definition' of change is perhaps this: changes are actualities of the second sort. While Socrates is actually becoming tanned he is still capable of becoming tanned (otherwise his tanning would get nowhere); while the hyacinth is actually growing, it is still capable of growing (otherwise it would be a poor, stunted plant); and in general, while an object is actually changing, it is still capable of changing.

Aristotle has much more to say about change. Change takes place in time and space, and the *Physics* offers intricate theories about the nature of time, of place, and of empty space. Since space and time are infinitely divisible, Aristotle analyses the notion of infinity. He also discusses a number of particular problems concerning the relation of motion to time, including a brief treatment of Zeno's celebrated paradoxes of motion.

The different essays which make up the *Physics* are among the more finished of Aristotle's surviving works: although their subject matter is thorny and although many passages of detailed argument are difficult, their general structure and purport are always clear. The *Physics* is one of the best places to start reading Aristotle.

Chapter 12
Causes

Material objects change, and their changes are caused. The scientist's world is full of causes, and scientific knowledge, as we have already seen, requires the capacity to state causes and to give explanations. We should expect Aristotle's scientific treatises to be filled with causal pronouncements and explanations, and we should expect his philosophical essays to include some account of the nature of causation and explanation. Neither expectation is disappointed.

The core of Aristotle's account of explanation is his doctrine of 'the four causes'. Here is his brief exposition:

> A thing is called a cause in one way if it is a constituent from which something comes to be (for example, bronze of the statue, silver of the goblet, and their genera); in another way if it is the form and pattern, that is, the formula of its essence, and the genera of this (for example, 2:1, and in general number, of the octave), and the parts present in the account; again, if it is the source of the first principle of change or rest (for example, the man who deliberates is a cause, and the father of the child, and in general the maker of what is being made and the changer of what is changing); again, if it is a goal – that is, that for the sake of which (for example, health of walking – Why is he walking? – we say: 'In order to be healthy', and in so saying we think we have stated the cause); and also those things which, when something else has initiated

a change, stand between the changer and the goal – for example, slimming or purging or drugs or instruments of health; for all these are for the sake of the goal, and they differ from one another in being some instruments and others actions.

Aristotle tells us that things are called 'causes' in four different ways, but his illustrations are brief and enigmatic. Consider the first example: 'bronze of the statue'. Aristotle can hardly mean that bronze explains, or is the cause of, the statue, since that makes no sense at all. But what does he mean? The first point to notice is that, in Aristotle's view, to ask for a cause is to seek 'the because-of-which'; that is to say, it is to ask why something is the case. A question 'Why?' requires an answer 'Because'; so if you want to cite the cause of something, you should be able to use a sentence of the form 'X because Y'.

Secondly, Aristotle says that 'the because-of-which is always sought in this way: Because of what does one thing belong to another? . . . for example: Because of what does it thunder? Because of what does noise occur in the clouds? For in this way one thing is being sought of another. Again: Because of what are these things, namely bricks and timbers, a house?' Whenever we seek a cause, we ask why this is that, why so-and-so is such-and-such. That is to say, the fact we are trying to explain can be expressed in a simple subject-predicate sentence: So-and-so is such-and-such. The question we ask is: Why is so-and-so such-and-such? And the answer can be put in the form: So-and-so is such-and-such because . . . (We can, of course, ask not only why wading-birds have webbed feet, but also why there are any wading-birds at all; and if the former question asks 'Because of what does one thing belong to another?', the latter question seems to be concerned with one thing only, namely wading-birds. Aristotle answers that point by appealing to his analysis of substances into matter and form: to ask why there are wading-birds is to ask why animal tissues sometimes have such-and-such a form – and that is to ask 'Because of what does one thing belong to another?')

84

14. 'A thing is called a cause in one way if it is a constituent from which something comes to be – for example, bronze of the statue.' A bronze statue from Delphi of a victorious charioteer.

Finally, Aristotle says that 'the cause is the middle term': to ask why so-and-so is such-and-such is, as it were, to look for a link joining so-and-so to such-and-such; and that link will constitute a 'middle term' between the two terms of the question. 'Why is so-and-so such-and-such?' – 'Because of so-and-such.' More fully: 'So-and-so is such-and-such, because so-and-so is so-and-such, and so-and-such is such-and-such.' Why do cows have several stomachs? Because cows are ruminants and ruminants have several stomachs. Explanations need not always actually be presented in that stiff form; but Aristotle holds that they always can be so presented, and that the stiff form exhibits the nature of causal connections most perspicuously.

This account of explanatory sentences enables us to see how Aristotle's notion of explanation is integrated with his logic, and how the causes which are the prime objects of the scientist's search may be expressed within the axiomatized deductive system which presents his finished product. Moreover, we are now better equipped to understand the doctrine of the 'four causes'.

'The constituent from which something comes to be', Aristotle's first type of cause, is usually called 'cause as matter' by him and 'the material cause' by his commentators. The illustration, 'bronze of the statue', is elliptical for something of the form: 'The statue is so-and-so because the statue is made of bronze and bronze things are so-and-so.' (Insert 'malleable', 'brown', 'heavy', 'covered in verdigris', etc. in place of 'so-and-so'.) The middle term, 'made of bronze', expresses the cause of the statue's being, for example, malleable; and because bronze is the constituent stuff of the statue the cause here is the material cause.

Aristotle's second sort of cause, 'the form and pattern', is normally referred to as the 'formal' cause. The illustration is again obscure. Consider instead the following passage: 'What it is and why it is are the same. What is an eclipse? – Privation of light from the moon by the earth's screening. Why is there an eclipse? or: Why is the moon eclipsed? – Because the light leaves it when the earth screens it.' In other words, the moon is eclipsed because the moon is deprived of light by being screened and things deprived of light by being screened are eclipsed. Here the middle term, 'deprived of light by being screened', explains why the eclipse occurs; and it states the form or essence of an eclipse – it says what an eclipse is.

Modern readers tend to associate the notion of causation most readily with the action of one thing on another – with pushings and pullings; and they may feel most at home with Aristotle's third type of cause, which is usually called the 'efficient' or 'motive' cause. At least, Aristotle's illustrations of the efficient cause have features which we now associate with the idea of causation. Thus the examples seem to suggest that efficient causes are distinct from the objects they operate upon (the father is distinct from the son, whereas the bronze is not distinct from the statue), and that causes precede their effects (the man who deliberates does so before he acts, whereas the screening does not occur before the eclipse).

Aristotle, however, does not regard efficient causes as radically different from material and formal causes. Moreover, he holds that efficient causes do not always precede their effects – indeed, he treats simultaneity of cause and effect as the normal case. His illustration, 'the father of the child', might be expanded as follows: 'The child is human because the child has a human father and children with human fathers are human.' Here the term which expresses the cause is 'having a human father'; and the cause does not precede the effect: the child does not first have a human father and then become human. Elsewhere Aristotle gives examples of antecedent causes: 'Why did the Persian War come upon the Athenians? What was the cause of the Athenians' being warred upon? – Because they attacked Sardis with the Eretrians; for that initiated the change.' But such examples are unusual.

Aristotle refers to his fourth cause as 'that for the sake of which' and 'the goal'. It is usually known as the 'final' cause ('*finis*' is the Latin for 'end' or 'goal'). The normal way of expressing final causes, as Aristotle's example indicates, is by using the connective 'in order to' or 'in order that': 'He is walking in order to be healthy.' Final causes are odd, in various ways: first, they are not readily expressed in terms of 'the because-of-which' – 'in order to' does not easily translate into 'because'. Secondly, they seem to be appropriate only to a very small number of cases, namely, human intentional actions (for 'in order to' expresses an intention, and only human actions are intentional). Thirdly, they appear to post-date their effects (health, which allegedly causes the walking, comes about after the walking). Fourthly, they may be effective without even existing (a man's health may cause him to walk and yet never come to exist – he may be too dissipated to become healthy, or he may be run over by a bus in the course of his perambulations).

The third and fourth oddities are the least troublesome. Aristotle explicitly recognizes that final causes follow their effects, and he implicitly acknowledges cases in which a final cause is effective but non-existent – neither point struck him as strange. The second oddity is more important. Aristotle does not think that final causes are appropriate only to intentional behaviour: on the contrary, the primary arena within which final causes exert themselves is that of nature – of the animal and vegetable world. I shall return to this point in a later chapter. The first oddity demands an immediate comment.

How do final causes fit Aristotle's account of the structure of explanatory sentences? One of his examples of a final cause is expressed concisely thus: 'Why is there a house? – In order to preserve a man's belongings.' We might expand the explanation as follows: Houses are roofed because houses are shelters for belongings and shelters for belongings are roofed. Here 'shelter for belongings' is the middle term, and it expresses the final cause of houses – it states the goal of having a house. But that gloss on Aristotle's illustration takes us some way from his text, and it is difficult to provide a similar gloss for the man who jogs for the sake of his health.

Final causes do not fit the 'such-and-such because so-and-such' formula. Perhaps we should relax things somewhat. 'Why is so-and-so such-and-such? Because of so-and-such.' In some cases, the relation of so-and-such to so-and-so and such-and-such will be as before: So-and-so is so-and-such, and so-and-such is such-and-such. In other cases, the relation may be more complex. In the case of final causes, so-and-such will explain why so-and-so is such-and-such inasmuch as so-and-such is both a goal for so-and-so and something achievable by way of such-and-such. 'Why does he walk? – For health': health is his goal; and health is achievable by walking. 'Why do ducks have webbed feet? – For swimming': swimming is a goal for ducks (that is, it is good for ducks to swim); and swimming is made easier by having webbed feet.

Aristotle's treatment of explanation contains much more than the distinction among four types of cause. I shall mention two further points. 'Since things are called causes in many ways, it happens that the same thing has many causes non-incidentally; for example, both the art of statue-making and the bronze are causes of the statue (not in virtue of something else, but *qua* statue); but not in the same way: one is cause in the sense of matter, the other in the sense of origin of change.' The same thing may have several different causes. It is tempting to construe 'the same thing' in a weak sense: the statue is heavy, say, because it is made of bronze; the statue is life-size because the sculptor made it so. The two causes are causes not of the very same feature of the statue, but rather of features of the very same statue. But that is not Aristotle's meaning; rather, he holds that one and the same feature of the statue may receive two distinct explanations, according to two different modes of causality. Thus he says that thunder occurs 'both because when fire is extinguished it necessarily sizzles and makes a noise and – if things are as the

Pythagoreans say – in order to threaten and frighten those in Hell'. And in the biological works he regularly looks for double causes in nature.

That is puzzling. Surely if one thing explains another, then there is no room for supposing that, in addition, some third thing explains it; if one thing accounts for another, then that item is accounted for – and there is no accounting left for a third item to do. It hardly makes any difference if the first and the third items pose as different types of cause. If we think we can give an adequate explanation of, say, the behaviour of a dog purely in mechanical terms (by a set of material and efficient causes), then we shall reject any further putative explanation in terms of the animal's goals or ends – such an attempt can explain nothing, since everything is already explained.

It is possible that Aristotle means something a little different from what he says: bronze may, in a way, be a cause of the statue's being heavy; but it is not by itself fully adequate to account for the weight of the statue – we need to add a reference to the sculptor, for he could quite well have fashioned a light statue out of bronze. The point, then, is not that something can be adequately explained by one item and also adequately explained by some different item; but rather that an adequate explanation of something may require mention of several different items. This is true; but it is not quite what Aristotle says.

Finally, a word about chance. Some of Aristotle's predecessors had ascribed numerous natural phenomena to chance, and Aristotle criticized them for so doing. Did he himself leave any room for chance in nature? He certainly believed, as we have already seen, that in nature many things happen not invariably but only for the most part. If something happens one way for the most part, then it must happen another way for the least part. Aristotle identifies 'the accidental' with such exceptions to what happens for the most part, with what happens for the least part. Thus for the most part, men go grey. But there are exceptions. Suppose that Socrates does not go grey: then that is an accident, and it may have occurred by chance. Aristotle adds that such accidental happenings are beyond the purview of science: 'And that there is no knowledge of the accidental is clear; for all knowledge deals either with what holds always or with what holds for the most part (for how else could one either learn it or teach it to someone else?).'

Thus in Aristotle's view, there are accidental phenomena in nature, and they are not subject to scientific knowledge. Does Aristotle infer that the world is to some extent indeterminate, that not all events are bound together by the nexus of causation? No – on the contrary, he supposes that the exceptions to natural regularities occur because of, and can be explained in terms of, peculiarities in the matter of the thing in question. If Socrates does not go grey, that is no causeless mystery: it is determined by the peculiar nature of Socrates' hair. Accidental phenomena have causes. Aristotle does not admit causeless events into the natural world. But he does allow that not all events are amenable to scientific understanding; for not everything exhibits the sort of regularity which science requires.

Chapter 13
Empiricism

How are we to acquire the knowledge which will eventually be packaged into neat Euclidean sciences? How do we get in touch with the substances which constitute the real world, and how do we chart their changes? How do we hit upon their causes and uncover their explanations? Deductive logic is not the answer: Aristotle's syllogistic was never supposed to be a means of finding out facts about the world – it provides a system within which knowledge can be articulated, not a device for making discoveries.

The ultimate source of knowledge, in Aristotle's view, is perception. Aristotle was a thoroughgoing 'empiricist' in two senses of that slippery term. First, he held that the notions or concepts in terms of which we seek to grasp and explain reality are all ultimately derived from perception; 'and for that reason, if we did not perceive anything, we would not learn or understand anything, and whenever we think of anything we must at the same time think of an idea'. Secondly, he thought that all science or knowledge is ultimately grounded on perceptual observations. This is perhaps hardly surprising: as a biologist, Aristotle's primary research tool was sense-perception, his own or that of others; as an ontologist, Aristotle's primary substances were ordinary perceptible objects. Plato, having given abstract Forms the leading role in his ontology, was led to regard the intellect rather than perception as the searchlight which illuminated reality. Aristotle, placing sensible particulars at the centre of the stage, took sense-perception as his torch.

Perception is the source of knowledge, but it is not knowledge itself. How, then, are the facts given in perception transformed into scientific knowledge? Aristotle describes the process as follows.

> All animals . . . have an innate capacity to make discriminations, which is called perception; and if perception is present in them, in some animals the percept is retained and in others it is not. Now for those in which it is not retained . . . there is no knowledge outside perception. But for some perceivers it is possible to hold the percept in their minds; and when many such things have come about there is a further difference, and some animals, from the retention of such things, come to possess a general account, while others do not. Thus from perception there comes memory, as we call it; and from memory (when it occurs often in connection with the same thing) experience – for memories that are many in number form a single experience; and from experience, or from the whole universal that has come to rest in the mind, . . . there comes a principle of skill and of knowledge.

We perceive particular facts – that this thing, here and now, is thus-and-so (that Socrates, say, is now going grey). That perception may stick in the mind and become a memory. Many of the facts we perceive are similar to one another: it is not just Socrates, but Callias and Plato and Nicomachus and the rest who are seen to go grey. And so we may come to have a batch of similar memories, the residues of similar perceptions. When we possess such a batch we have what Aristotle terms 'experience'; and experience is turned into something very close to knowledge when 'the whole universal has come to rest in the mind', when the batch of particular memories is, as it were, compressed into a single thought – the thought that, for the most part, all men go grey. (I say 'something very close to knowledge': knowledge itself does not arrive until we grasp the cause of greying –

until we learn that men go grey as they grow old because as they grow old the sources of pigmentation dry up.) Knowledge, in sum, is bred by generalization out of perception.

This story is open to criticism. First, it is clear that most of our knowledge is not acquired in the way Aristotle suggests. We do not normally require a mass of similar observations before we jump to a universal judgement: I doubt if Aristotle observed hectocotylization in more than one or two octopuses, and he surely dissected very few prawns before giving his general description of their internal parts. The story he tells of the growth of general knowledge from particular observations may be correct at bottom, but its plot must be considerably refined if it is to be an adequate account of our actual procedures.

Secondly, Aristotle's story will meet a philosophical challenge. Is sense-perception reliable? If so, how can we tell that it is? How can we distinguish illusion from genuine perception? And again, are we justified in moving from particular observations to general truths? How can we know if we have made enough observations or if our actual observations are a fair sample of the field of possible observations? Questions of this sort have been asked by sceptically minded philosophers for centuries, and they need to be addressed by any serious Aristotelian.

Aristotle was aware of the dangers of hasty generalization; for example, 'the cause of the ignorance of those who take this view is that, while the differences among animals with regard to copulation and procreation are manifold and unobvious, these people observe a few cases and think that things must be the same in all cases'. But Aristotle has nothing to say in general terms about the problems raised by generalization: those problems – problems of 'induction' as they were later called – did not receive detailed philosophical attention until long after Aristotle's death. Aristotle has rather more to say about the

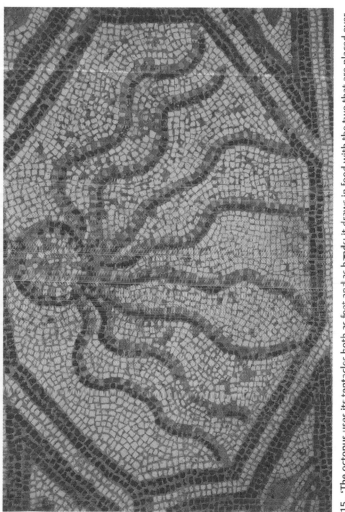

15. 'The octopus uses its tentacles both as feet and as hands: it draws in food with the two that are placed over its mouth; and the last of its tentacles . . . it uses for copulation.'

problems of perception. In his psychological treatise *On the Soul* he remarks in passing that the reliability of the senses varies according to the objects at which they are directed. If our eyes tell us 'That is white' they are most unlikely to be wrong; if they say 'That white thing is a daisy' they have a greater chance of erring. And Book IV of the *Metaphysics* considers and dismisses a number of sceptical positions. But the remarks in *On the Soul* are not backed by any argument, and Aristotle's reply to the sceptics in the *Metaphysics* is little more than a curt dismissal. He thinks that their views are not seriously held and need not be seriously taken: 'it is evident that no one – neither those who state the thesis nor anyone else – is actually in that condition. For why does anyone walk to Megara rather than stay where he is when he thinks he should walk there? Why doesn't he walk into a well or over a cliff in the morning if there is one about?' And Aristotle asks if 'they are really puzzled as to whether sizes and colours are such as they seem to those at a distance or to those who are near, to the healthy or to the sick; whether what seems heavy to the weak or to the strong really is heavy; whether what seems to be the case to men awake or to men asleep really is true'.

If someone assures me that we can know nothing at all about the world, and I then see him looking carefully in each direction before he crosses the road, I shall not take his assurance seriously. And in general, sceptical assurances are shown in this sort of way to be unserious. Perhaps this is so; but it is hardly pertinent to the philosophical questions which Aristotle's optimistic epistemology encounters. A sceptic's arguments may be serious even if he is not. A sceptic's objections may be pointed, and may demand a response, even if the sceptic is a playboy. Aristotle ought perhaps to have taken scepticism more seriously – but he had to leave bones for his successors to gnaw.

Chapter 14
Aristotle's World-Picture

Aristotle was an industrious collector who amassed a prodigious quantity of information on a vast variety of topics. He was also an abstract thinker, whose philosophical ideas ranged wide. The two aspects of his intellectual activity were not kept in distinct mental compartments. On the contrary, Aristotle's scientific work and his philosophical investigations were the two halves of a unified intellectual outlook. Aristotle was a remarkable scientist and a profound philosopher, but it is as a philosopher-scientist that he excels. He was, according to an ancient aphorism, 'a scribe of nature who dipped his pen in thought'.

His main philosophico-scientific writings are the *Physics*, *On Generation and Destruction*, *On the Heavens*, *Meteorology*, *On the Soul*, the collection of short psychological treatises known collectively as the *Parva Naturalia*, the *Parts of Animals*, and the *Generation of Animals*. All these works are scientific, in the sense that they are based on empirical research, and attempt to organize and explain the observed phenomena. They are also all philosophical, in the sense that they are acutely self-conscious, reflective, and systematically structured attempts to arrive at the truth of things.

Aristotle himself indicates the general plan of his work at the beginning of the *Meteorology*.

I have already dealt with the first causes of nature and with all natural motion [in the *Physics*], and also with the heavenly bodies arranged in their upper paths [in *On the Heavens*], and with the number and nature of the material elements, with their mutual transformations, and with generation and destruction in general [in *On Generation and Corruption*]. The part of this enquiry remaining to be considered is what all the earlier thinkers called meteorology ... When we have dealt with these subjects, we shall see if we can give some account, on the lines we have laid down, of animals and plants, both in general and in particular; for when we have done that, we shall perhaps have arrived at the completion of the plan we set ourselves at the beginning.

Aristotle offers a clear view of the nature of reality. The elements or fundamental stuffs of the sublunary world are four: earth, air, fire, and water. Each element is defined by way of four primary powers or qualities – wetness, dryness, coldness, hotness. (Fire is hot and dry, earth cold and dry, . . .) The elements have each a natural movement and a natural place. Fire, if left to itself, will move upwards and will find its place at the outermost edges of the universe; earth naturally moves downwards, to the centre of the universe; air and water find their places in between. The elements can act upon and change into one another. Elemental interactions are discussed in *On Generation and Destruction*; secondary forms of interaction – something approximating to chemistry – may be found in Book IV of the *Meteorology*.

Earth tends downwards, and our earth is naturally at the centre of the universe. Beyond the earth and its atmosphere come the moon, the sun, the planets, and the fixed stars. Aristotle's geocentric astronomy, which attaches the heavenly bodies to a series of concentric spheres, was not his own creation. He was not a professional astronomer but relied upon the work of his contemporaries, Eudoxus and Callippus. The treatise *On the Heavens* is concerned with abstract astronomy.

16. A thirteenth-century painting of the Aristotelian elements: 'The elements or fundamental stuffs of the sublunary world are four: earth, air, fire, and water. Each element is defined by way of four primary powers or qualities – wetness, dryness, coldness, hotness.'

Aristotle's main contention is that the physical universe is spatially finite but temporally infinite: it is a vast but bounded sphere which has existed without beginning and will exist without end.

Between the earth and the moon lies the mid-air. The *Meteorology* studies '*ta meteôra*', literally 'the things suspended in mid-air'. The phrase referred originally to such phenomena as clouds, thunder, rain, snow, frost, dew – roughly speaking, to the weather; but it was easily extended to include matters which we should classify under astronomy (meteors, comets, the milky way, for example) or under geography (rivers, the sea, mountains, etc.). Aristotle's *Meteorology* contains his own explanations of these various phenomena. The work has a strong empirical base, but it is firmly governed by theory. Indeed, the unity which it possesses derives largely from the dominance of a single theoretical notion, the notion of 'exhalation'. Aristotle holds that 'exhalations' or evaporations are continuously being given off by the earth. They are of two sorts, wet or steamy, and dry or smoky. Their actions may serve to explain, in a uniform fashion, most of the events that take place in the mid-air.

On the earth itself the most remarkable objects of study are living things and their parts. 'Of the parts in animals, some are incomposite, namely those which divide into uniform pieces (for example, flesh into flesh), others are composite, namely those which divide into non-uniform pieces (for example, a hand does not divide into hands, nor a face into faces) . . . All the non-uniform parts are composed from the uniform parts, for example, hands from flesh and sinews and bones.' But there is no sharp boundary between non-living and living things; and although living things can be arranged in a hierarchy – a 'ladder of nature' of ascending worth and complexity – the levels in the hierarchy are not rigorously separated. Between plants and the lowest form of animals there is no precise boundary; and from the lowest animals to men, who naturally stand at the top of the ladder, there is a continuous progression.

Such is the natural world. And as such it continues forever, exhibiting constant regularity in continuous change.

> Circular motion, that is, the motion of the heavens, has been seen . . . to be eternal, because it and the motions determined by it come into being and will exist from necessity. For if that which moves in a circle is always moving something else, the motion of the latter too must be circular – for example, since the upper movement is circular, the sun moves in this way; and since this is so, the seasons for that reason come into being in a circle and return upon themselves; and since they come into being in this way, so again do the things governed by them.

And how is the world governed? Are there gods to keep it going? Outwardly Aristotle was a conventional polytheist; at least, in his will he ordered statues to be dedicated at Stagira to Zeus and to Athena. But such ritual performances did not mirror his philosophical beliefs:

> Our remote ancestors have handed down remnants to their posterity in mythical form to the effect that these [sc. the heavenly bodies] are gods and that the divine encompasses the whole of nature. But the rest has been added by way of myth to persuade the vulgar and for the use of the laws and of expediency. For they say that they are anthropomorphic and like some of the other animals – and other things consequent upon and similar to that; but if you were to separate what they say and accept only the first part, that they thought the primary substances to be gods, you would think they had spoken divinely.

Zeus and Athena, the anthropomorphic gods of the Olympian pantheon, are myths; but 'our remote ancestors' were not purveyors of unmixed superstition. They rightly saw, or half saw, first that the 'primary substances' are divine ('god seems to everyone to be among the causes and a sort of first principle'), and secondly that the primary substances should be sought in the heavens.

The heavenly bodies, which Aristotle often refers to as 'the divine bodies', are made of a special stuff, a fifth element or 'quintessence'; for 'there is some other body, separate from those here about us, whose nature is more honourable in that it is further removed from the world below'. Now 'it is the function of what is most divine to think and to use its intellect', so that the heavenly bodies, being divine, must therefore be alive and intelligent. For although 'we tend to think of them as though they were simply bodies – units exhibiting order but quite without life – we must suppose that they partake in action and in life . . . We must think that the actions of the stars are just like those of animals and plants.'

In Book VIII of the *Physics* Aristotle argues for the existence of a changeless source of change – an 'unmoved mover' as it is normally called. If there is to be any change in the universe, there must, he holds, be some original source which imparts change to other things without changing itself. The unmoved mover is outside the universe: 'must there or must there not be something unchanging and at rest outside whatever is changing and no part of it? And must this be true of the universe too? It would presumably seem absurd if the principle of change were inside it.' The external mover 'initiates change as an object of love; and other things initiate change by changing themselves'. The concentric celestial spheres, and the celestial bodies they carry, are all quintessential and divine; but they are moving divinities. Beyond them, incorporeal and outside the universe, is the primary divinity, the changeless originator of all change.

What are we to make of all this? Some scholars take Aristotle's words at what seems to be their face value, and find living gods scattered throughout his writings – he thus becomes a profoundly religious scientist. Other scholars dismiss Aristotle's use of the words 'god' and 'divine' as a *façon de parler*: the primary substances are divine only in the sense that other things are dependent upon them – and Aristotle becomes a wholly secular thinker.

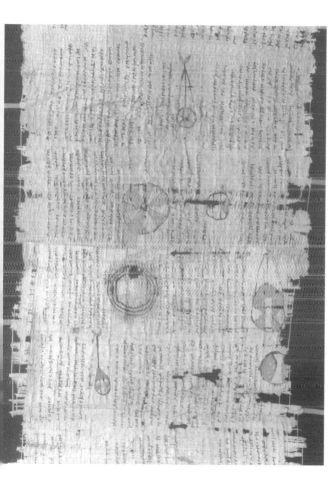

17. 'Aristotle's geocentric astronomy, which attaches the heavenly bodies to a series of concentric spheres, was not his own creation. He was not a professional astronomer but relied upon the work of his contemporaries, Eudoxus and Callippus.' Part of a papyrus text (from the second century AD) of Eudoxus' work On Spheres.

Neither of those two views is plausible. There is too much about gods in the treatises to permit us to discount Aristotle's theologizing as pious word play; and, on the other hand, Aristotle's gods are too abstract, remote, and impersonal to be regarded as the objects of religious worship. Rather, we might connect Aristotle's remarks about the divinity of the universe with the sense of wonderment which nature and its works produced in him. 'It is because of wonderment that men, both now and at first, start to study philosophy'; and that study, properly conducted, does not diminish the initial admiration. For Aristotle was impressed by a deep reverence for the value and excellence of the universe about him:

> In what way does the nature of the world contain what is good and what is best – as something separate and independent, or as its own orderliness? Rather, in both ways, as an army does. For the excellence of an army resides both in its orderliness and in its general, and especially in the latter. For he does not depend on the orderliness but it does depend on him. And all things – fish and birds and plants – are ordered in a way, yet not in the same way; and it is not the case that there is no connection between one thing and another – there is a connection.

Chapter 15
Psychology

One important distinction within the natural world is found in the fact that some natural substances are alive and others inanimate. What marks off the former from the latter is their possession of what in Greek is called *psuchê*. The word '*psuchê*' (from which 'psychology' and other such terms derive) is usually translated as 'soul', and under the heading of *psuchê* Aristotle does indeed include those features of the higher animals which later thinkers associate with the soul. But 'soul' is a misleading translation. It is a truism that all living things – prawns and pansies no less than men and gods – possess a *psuchê*; but it would be odd to suggest that a prawn has a soul, and odder still to ascribe souls to pansies. Since a *psuchê* is what animates, or gives life to, a living thing, the word 'animator' (despite its overtones of Disneyland) might be used. (I shall generally keep to the conventional 'soul', but I shall also occasionally use 'animator'.)

Souls or animators come in varying degrees of complexity.

> Some things possess all the powers of the soul, others some of them, others one only. The powers we mentioned were those of nutrition, of perception, of appetition, of change in place, of thought. Plants possess only the nutritive power. Other things possess both that and the power of perception. And if the power of perception, then that of appetition too. For appetition consists of desire, inclination, and wish; all animals

possess at least one of the senses, namely touch; everything which has perception also experiences pleasure and pain, the pleasant and the painful; and everything which experiences those also possesses desire (for desire is appetition for the pleasant) . . . Some things possess in addition to these the power of locomotion; and others also possess the power of thought and intelligence.

Thought, in Aristotle's view, requires imagination and hence perception; so that any thinking creature must be capable of perceiving. And perception never exists apart from the first principle of animation, that of nutrition and reproduction. Thus the various powers or faculties of the soul form a hierarchical system.

What is a soul or animator? And how do living creatures acquire one?

Aristotle

In his treatise *On the Soul* Aristotle offers a general account of what souls or animators are. He first argues that 'if we are to state something common to every type of soul, it will be that it is the first fulfilment of a natural body which has organs'. He later observes that such an account is not particularly illuminating, and suggests, as an improvement, that 'a soul is a principle of the aforesaid powers and is defined by them, namely by nutrition, perception, thought, movement'. Aristotle himself advises us not to spend too much time over these generalities but rather to concentrate on the different functions of the soul.

Yet the generalities contain something of importance. Aristotle's first general account of the soul amounts to this: for a thing to have a soul is for it to be a natural organic body actually capable of functioning. The second general account explains what those functions are. Thus Aristotle's souls are not pieces of living things, nor are they bits of spiritual stuff placed inside physical bodies; rather, they are sets of powers, sets of capacities or faculties. Possessing a soul is like possessing a skill. A carpenter's skill is not some part of him, responsible for his skilled acts; similarly, a living creature's animator or soul is not some part of it, responsible for its living activities.

This view of the soul has certain consequences, which Aristotle was quick to draw. First, 'one should not ask if the soul and the body are one, any more than one should ask such a question of a piece of wax and its shape or in general of the matter of anything and that of which it is the matter'. There is no problem of the 'unity' of soul and body, or of how soul and body can act upon each other. Descartes later wondered how on earth two things so different as body and soul could coexist and work together; for Aristotle such issues do not arise.

Secondly, 'that the soul – or certain parts of it, if it is divisible into parts – is not separable from the body is not unclear'. Fulfilments cannot exist apart from the things that are fulfilled. Souls are fulfilments of bodies. Hence souls cannot exist apart from bodies, any more than skills can exist apart from skilled men. Plato had held that souls pre-existed the birth and survived the death of those bodies they animated. Aristotle thought that this was impossible. A soul is simply not the sort of thing that could survive. How could my skills, my temper, or my character survive me?

Aristotle's general view of the nature of souls is elaborated in his detailed accounts of the different life-functions: nutrition, reproduction, perception, movement, thought. Such functions or faculties are functions or faculties of bodies, and Aristotle's psychological investigations can take a biological turn without, as it were, changing the subject. Thus imagination, for example, is described as 'a motion coming about by the agency of an act of perception': an act of perception is a physiological change, and it may cause a further physiological change, which constitutes an imagination. Some may object that Aristotle ignores the psychological aspect of imagination by concentrating on its physiological manifestations. But Aristotle holds that the psychology simply is the physiology, that souls and their parts are physical capacities.

On the Soul and the *Parva Naturalia* are governed by this biological attitude towards animation. In the *Generation of Animals* Aristotle asks where the soul or animator comes from: how do creatures begin to live? A popular view, accepted by Plato, had it that life begins when the soul enters the body. Aristotle comments: 'clearly, those principles whose actuality is corporeal cannot exist without a body – for example, walking without feet; hence they cannot come in from outside – for they cannot enter it alone (for they are inseparable), nor yet in some body (for the semen is a residue of food that is undergoing change).' The 'principles' or powers of the soul are corporeal principles – to be animated is to be a body with certain capacities. Hence to suppose that those capacities could exist outside any body is as absurd as to imagine that walking could take place apart from any legs. The soul cannot simply drift into the foetus from outside. (In principle, it could arrive 'in some body', that is, in the semen; but in fact the semen is the wrong sort of stuff to carry or transmit these capacities.)

Aristotle's accounts of nutrition, reproduction, perception, desire, and movement are all consistently biological. But consistency is threatened when he turns to the highest psychological faculty, that of thought. In the *Generation of Animals*, immediately after the sentences just quoted, Aristotle continues: 'Hence it remains that thought alone comes in from outside, and that it alone is divine; for corporeal actuality has no connection at all with the actuality of thought.' Thought, it seems, can exist apart from body. The treatise *On the Soul* speaks of thought with special caution, hinting that it may be separable from body. In what is perhaps the most perplexing paragraph he ever wrote, Aristotle distinguishes between two sorts of thought (later known as 'active intellect' and 'passive intellect'). Of the first of these he says: 'this thought is separable and impassive and unmixed, being essentially actuality . . . And when separated it is just what it is, and it alone is immortal and eternal.'

The special status of thought depends upon the view that thinking does not involve any corporeal activity. But how can Aristotle hold such a view? His general account of the soul makes it plain that thinking is something done by 'natural organic bodies', and his particular analysis of the nature of thought makes thinking dependent upon imagination and hence upon perception. Even if thinking is not itself a corporeal activity, it requires other corporeal activities in order to take place.

Aristotle's treatment of thought is both obscure in itself and hard to reconcile with the rest of his psychology. But neither that fact, nor the various errors and inexactitudes in his physiology, should dim the light of his work on psychology: it rests on a subtle insight into the nature of souls or animators, and it is persistently scientific in its approach to psychological questions.

Chapter 16
Evidence and Theory

Aristotle's general account of the world is wholly exploded. Most of his explanations are now seen to be false. Many of the concepts he operated with appear crude and inadequate. Some of his ideas seem quite absurd. The chief reason for Aristotle's downfall is simple: in the sixteenth and seventeenth centuries, scientists applied quantitative methods to the study of inanimate nature, and chemistry and physics came to assume a dominating role. Those two sciences seemed to be fundamental in a way in which biology was not: they examined the same stuff as biology, but from a closer, and a mathematical, view-point – a biology unsupported by physics and chemistry was seen to lack a foundation. Aristotle's physics and chemistry were found to be hopelessly inadequate when compared to the work of the new scientists. A new 'world-picture', based on the new sciences, replaced the Aristotelian view, and if Aristotle's biology survived for a further century or so, it survived as a limb torn from the body, as a fragment of a colossal statue.

Why did Aristotle not develop a decent chemistry or an adequate physics? His failing must be set down in large part to conceptual poverty. He did not have our concepts of mass, force, velocity, temperature, and he thus lacked some of the most powerful conceptual tools of the physical sciences. In some cases he had a rough and primitive form of the concept – he knew what speed was, and he could weigh things. But his notion of speed is in a sense non-quantitative; for he did not measure velocity, he had no notion of kilometres per hour. Or again, consider temperature. Heat is a central notion in Aristotelian science. The hot and the cold are two of the four primary powers, and heat is vital to animal life. Aristotle's predecessors had disagreed among themselves over what objects were hot and what cold. 'If there is so much dispute over the hot and the cold,' Aristotle remarks, 'what must we think about the rest? – for these are the clearest of the things we perceive'. He suspects that the disputes occur 'because the term "hotter" is used in several ways', and he conducts a long analysis of the different criteria we use for calling things hot. The analysis is subtle, but – to our eyes – it suffers from a glaring deficiency: it does not mention measurement. For Aristotle, hotness is a matter of degree, but not of measurable degree. To that extent he lacked the notion of temperature.

Conceptual poverty is closely tied to technological poverty. Aristotle had no accurate clock, and no thermometer at all. Measuring devices and a quantitative conceptual apparatus go together. The former are inconceivable without the latter, the latter are useless without the former. Lacking one, Aristotle lacked both. In an earlier chapter I suggested that Aristotle's zoological researches did not suffer from his non-quantitative approach. The case is different with the natural sciences: chemistry without laboratory equipment and physics without mathematics are bad chemistry and bad physics.

It would be absurd to blame Aristotle for his conceptual poverty: poverty is a lack, not a failing. But many students of Aristotle's science are inclined to impute two serious failings to him, one methodological and the other substantial. It is alleged, first, that Aristotle regularly subordinated fact to theory, that he would start from theory, and then twist the facts to fit it; and secondly, that his natural science was permeated by a childlike determination to find plans and purposes in the world of nature. Let us take the methodological accusation first.

Consider the following passage:

> we might say that plants belong to earth, aquatic animals to water, land-animals to air . . . The fourth kind must not be looked for in these regions; yet there should be a kind corresponding to the position of fire – for this is reckoned the fourth of the bodies . . . But such a kind must be sought on the moon; for that evidently shares in the fourth remove – but that is matter for another treatise.

The passage comes in the middle of a sophisticated and informed discussion of certain questions of generation. It would be charitable to regard it as a joke; but it is not in the least jocular: Aristotle convinces himself that there are kinds of animals corresponding to three of his four elements; he infers that there must be a kind corresponding to the fourth element; and, failing to find such things on the earth, he places them on the moon. What could be more absurd? What less scientific?

Well, the passage is absurd; and there are one or two others to match it. But all scientists are capable of idiocy: there are remarkably few idiotic passages in Aristotle's writings, and the judicious reader will not make too much of them. Rather, he will find other passages more characteristic of the man. For example, speaking of the motions of the heavenly bodies, Aristotle writes:

> as to how many there are, let us now say what some of the mathematicians say, in order to get some idea of the matter and so that our mind will have some definite number to grasp hold of. As to the future, we must make enquiries ourselves and discuss the matter with other enquirers, and if those who study these matters have views different from those now expressed, we must love both parties but listen to the more accurate.

Again: 'to judge by argument and by the facts which seem to hold about them, the generation of bees takes place in this manner. But we have not yet acquired an adequate grasp of the facts: if we ever do acquire such a grasp, we must then rely on perception rather than on arguments – and on arguments only if what they prove is in agreement with the phenomena.' Aristotle has just given a long and careful account of the generation of bees. The account is based primarily on observations; but it is also speculative, relying to some extent on theoretical considerations. Aristotle explicitly recognizes this speculative aspect of his account, and he explicitly holds that speculation is subordinate to observation. Theory is indispensable when the facts are insufficiently known, but observation always has priority over theory.

Aristotle elsewhere makes the same point in more general terms: 'We must first grasp the differences between animals and the facts about them all. After that, we must try to discover their causes. For that is the natural method of procedure, once the research about each of them is done; for from that will become apparent the subjects about which and the principles from which our proofs must be conducted.' Again:

> empirical science must pass down the principles – I mean, for example, empirical astronomy must supply those of the science of astronomy; for when the phenomena were sufficiently grasped, the astronomical proofs were discovered. And similarly in every other art and science whatsoever. Thus if the facts in each case are grasped, it will then be our task to give a ready supply of proofs. For if none of the true facts of the case is missing, we shall be able to discover the proof of everything of which there is proof and to construct a proof – and to make plain where proof is not possible.

Aristotle frequently criticizes his predecessors for putting theory before the facts. Thus, of Plato and his school:

> speaking of the phenomena, they say things that do not agree with the

18. 'To judge by argument and by the facts which seem to hold about them, the generation of bees takes place in the way we have described. But we have not yet acquired an adequate grasp of the facts . . .'

phenomena . . . They are so fond of their first principles that they seem to behave like those who defend theses in dialectical arguments; for they accept any consequence, thinking that they have true principles – as though principles should not be judged by their consequences, and especially by their goal. And the goal in productive science is the product, but in natural science it is whatever properly appears to perception.

Nothing could be clearer. Empirical research precedes theory. The facts must be collected before the causes are sought. The construction of an axiomatized deductive science (the production of proofs) depends upon the presence of 'all the true facts of the case'. Of course, Aristotle never had a grasp of all the facts; he often thought he had facts when he had only falsehoods; and he sometimes jumped precipitately into theorizing. Moreover, theory should to some extent control the collection of facts: undisciplined amassing of facts is an unscientific exercise; and it may be, as some philosophers both ancient and modern have argued, that there is no such thing as a pure fact uncontaminated by theory. But despite all this, two things are plain: Aristotle had a clear view of the primacy of observation, and his scientific treatises – in particular, his works on biology – regularly remain true to that view.

In the next chapter I turn to the accusation that Aristotle childishly makes the natural world a stage on which plans and purposes are acted out

Chapter 17
Teleology

> We see more than one kind of cause concerned with natural generation
> – namely that for the sake of which, and also the source of the principle
> of change. Thus we must determine which of these comes first and
> which second. It seems that the first is the one we call 'for the sake of
> something'; for this is the account of the thing, and the account is a
> principle in the same way both in the products of skill and in those of
> nature. For, either by thought or by perception, the doctor determines
> on health and the builder on a house; and then they give accounts and
> causes of everything they do, and explain why it should be done in this
> way. Now that for the sake of which, or the good, is more prevalent in
> the works of nature than in those of skill.

Here, in the introductory chapter of the *Parts of Animals*, Aristotle sets
out what is called his teleological view of nature. Final causes occur in
the works of nature no less than in the products of human skill, and in
order to explain natural phenomena we must appeal to 'that for the
sake of which'. Explanation in terms of final causes is explanation in
terms of 'the good'; for if ducks have webbed feet for the sake of
swimming, then it is good – that is, good for ducks – to have webbed
feet. Final causes are primary because they are identified with 'the
account of the thing': being a swimmer is part of a duck's essence, and
a proper account of what it is to be a duck will require reference to

swimming. Final causes are not imposed on nature by theoretical considerations; they are observed in nature: 'we see more than one kind of cause'. (The term 'teleology' derives from the Greek 'telos', which is Aristotle's word for 'goal': a teleological explanation is one which appeals to goals or final causes.)

Throughout his biological works Aristotle constantly looks for final causes. Why do teeth, unlike the other hard parts of animal structure, continue to grow?

> The cause of their growth, in the sense of that for the sake of which, is to be found in their function. For they would soon be worn away if there were no accretion to them – as it is, in certain old animals which are gross feeders but possess small teeth, the teeth are completely worn away, for they are destroyed more quickly than they grow. That is why here too nature has produced an excellent contrivance to fit the case; for she makes loss of the teeth coincide with old age and death. If life lasted for ten thousand or one thousand years, the teeth would have had to be enormous at first and to grow up often; for even if they grew continuously, they would nevertheless be smoothed down and so become useless for their work. So much for that for the sake of which they grow.

Again, why do men have hands?

> Anaxagoras says that men are the most intelligent of animals because they possess hands; but it is reasonable to think that they possess hands because they are most intelligent. For hands are a tool, and nature, like an intelligent man, always assigns each thing to something that can use it (it is better to give a flute to someone who is actually a flute-player than to provide a man who owns a flute with the skill of flute-playing); for she has provided the greater and superior thing with that which is less, and not the less with that which is more honourable and greater. Thus if this is better, and if nature does what is the best in the

circumstances, man is not most intelligent because of his hands but has hands because he is the most intelligent of animals.

Final causes are often contrasted with 'necessity', and in particular with the constraints imposed by the material nature of animals or animal parts. But even where necessity is invoked to explain the phenomena, there is still room for explanation in terms of final causes. Why do water-birds have webbed feet?

> For these causes, they have them from necessity; and because of what is better, they have such feet for the sake of life, so that, living in the water where their wings are useless, they may have feet that are useful for swimming. For they are like oars to oarsmen or fins to fish; hence if in fish the fins are destroyed or in water-birds the webbing between the feet, they no longer swim.

Aristotle's teleology is sometimes summed up in the slogan 'Nature does nothing in vain', and he himself frequently uses aphorisms of this tenor. But although Aristotle holds that final causes are to be found throughout the natural world, they are not to be found literally everywhere. 'The bile in the liver is a residue, and is not for the sake of anything – like the sediment in the stomach and in the intestines. Now nature sometimes uses even residues for some advantageous purpose; but that is no reason for seeking a final cause in all cases.' Book V of the *Generation of Animals* is entirely devoted to such non-purposeful parts of animals.

Natural behaviour and natural structure usually have final causes; for nature does nothing in vain. But the final causes are constrained by necessity: nature does the best she can 'in the circumstances'. And sometimes there is no final cause to be discovered at all.

The *Physics* contains a number of arguments in support of natural teleology. Some of them rest upon the characteristically Aristotelian notion that 'art imitates nature' or 'the arts are imitations of nature': if we can see final causes in the products of skill, all the more so can we see them in the products of nature. Another argument enlarges upon the assertion in the *Parts of Animals* that 'we see' final causes in nature.

> It is particularly clear in the case of the other animals which act neither by skill nor after enquiry nor after deliberation (hence some people wonder whether spiders, ants, and the like perform their tasks by reason or by something else). And if you proceed little by little in this way, it becomes apparent that in plants too there occurs what is conducive to the goal – for example, leaves for the sake of sheltering the fruit. So that if the swallow builds its nest and the spider its web by nature and for the sake of something, and if plants too produce leaves for the sake of the fruit and grow their roots downwards rather than upwards for the sake of nutrition, it is plain that there are causes of this sort in the things that come to be and exist by nature.

Do we 'see' final causes in nature? What exactly are we supposed to see? The phrases 'in order to' and 'for the sake of' seem to be primarily of service in explaining the intentional actions of conscious agents. Then is Aristotle ascribing agency and intentionality to natural phenomena? He does not attribute intentions to animals and plants, nor does he suppose that the final causes of their activities are what they themselves purpose. Ducks do not plan to have webbed feet, nor do plants contrive their leaves. Aristotle's teleology does not consist in a puerile ascription of intentions to vegetables. Then is Aristotle attributing intentions not to natural creatures but to nature herself? In several passages Aristotle speaks of nature as the intelligent artificer of the natural world, passages in which we are inclined to write 'Nature' with a capital N. For example, 'like a good housekeeper, nature does not waste anything which might be put to good use.' Such passages should not be lightly dismissed. But nature the artificer cannot be all that there is to Aristotle's teleology; for in the detailed teleological explanations which fill his biological writings he rarely adverts to the plans of nature or to the purposes of a grand designer.

If we are not to interpret Aristotle's teleology in terms of intentional planning, how are to interpret it? Consider the following passage.

> Snakes copulate by twining around one another; and they have no testicles and no penis, as I have already observed – no penis because they have no legs, no testicles . . . because of their length. For because they are naturally elongated, if there were further delay in the region of the testicles, the semen would grow cool because of its slow passage. (This happens in the case of men who have large penises: they are less fertile than those with moderate penises because cold semen is not fertile and semen that is carried a long way cools.)

If the snake's semen had to wind its way through a pair of testicles after travelling the length of the snake's body, it would become cold and infertile – and that is why snakes have no testicles. (They have no penis because the penis is naturally located between the legs, and snakes have no legs.) In order to procreate successfully, snakes must lack testicles: they would not survive if they did not procreate, and they could not procreate if they had testicles. That explains their lack of testicles. The explanation is fantastical in its content, but it is an explanation of a perfectly respectable type.

In general, most structural features and behavioural traits of animals and plants have a function. That is to say, they serve the performance of some activity which is essential, or at least useful, to the organism: if the organism did not perform that activity it would not survive at all, or would only survive with difficulty. If we are seeking an understanding of animal life, we must grasp the functions associated with the creature's parts and behaviour. If you know that ducks have webbed feet and also know that they swim, you are not yet in possession of full understanding: you need to grasp in addition that the

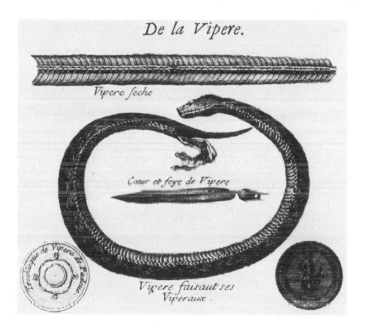

De la Vipere.

Vipere seche

Coeur et foye de Vipere

Trochique de Vipere le Pasten

Vipere faisant ses Viperaux.

19. 'Snakes copulate by twining around one another; and they have no testicles and no penis, as I have already observed – no penis because they have no leqs, no testicles . . . because of their lenqth.'

webbing helps ducks to swim, and that swimming is an essential part of the duck's life.

Aristotle expresses this by saying that one answer to the question 'Why do ducks have webbed feet?' is 'In order to swim.' His 'in order to' sounds odd to us only because we associate 'in order to' primarily with intentional action. Aristotle associates it primarily with function, and he sees function in nature. He is surely right. Natural objects do contain functional parts and do exhibit functional behaviour; the scientist who is unaware of such functions is ignorant of a major part of his subject-matter.

'Nature does nothing in vain' is a regulative principle for scientific enquiry. Aristotle knows that some aspects of nature are functionless. But he recognizes that a grasp of function is crucial to an understanding of nature. His slogans about the prudence of nature are not pieces of childish superstition, but reminders of a central task of the natural scientist.

Chapter 18
Practical Philosophy

The preceding chapters have been concerned with the theoretical sciences. Aristotle himself devoted most of his time to that great branch of knowledge, but he did not ignore the practical sciences. Indeed, two of his most celebrated treatises, the *Politics* and the *Nicomachean Ethics*, belong to the practical branch of philosophy. Those works are not practical in the sense of being manuals. On the contrary, they are full of analysis and argument, and they rest upon much historical and scientific research. They are works of practical philosophy, practical in the sense that their purpose or aim is not merely to purvey truth but also to affect action: 'the present treatise is not, like the others, undertaken for the sake of understanding – for we are conducting the enquiry not in order to know what goodness is but in order to become good men'.

Aristotle wrote two *Ethics*, the *Nicomachean* and the *Eudemian*. The title '*Ethics*' is misleading, and so too are the standard English translations of two key terms in Aristotle's practical philosophy – '*aretê*', normally rendered 'virtue', and '*eudaimonia*', normally rendered 'happiness'. A few remarks on these words are in order.

Aristotle himself refers to his treatises as the '*êthika*', and the transliteration of the Greek word gives us the title '*Ethics*'. But the Greek term actually means 'matters to do with character', and a better title would be *On Matters of Character*. As for '*aretê*', the word means something like 'goodness' or 'excellence': Aristotle can talk of the *aretê* of an argument or of an axe as well as of a man. Human *aretê* is human excellence: it is what makes a human being a good human being; and it has only an indirect connection with what we think of as virtue. Finally, '*eudaimonia*' does not refer to a mental state of euphoria, as 'happiness' tends to in English: to be *eudaimôn* is to flourish, to make a success of life, and the connection between *eudaimonia* and happiness is again indirect.

What, then, is Aristotle's 'ethical' philosophy? 'It seems no doubt uncontroversial to say that *eudaimonia* is the best thing, but we need to say more clearly what it is.' Each of us wants to flourish or to do well, and all our actions, in so far as they are rational, are directed to that ultimate goal. The primary question for practical philosophy, then, is this: How are we to achieve *eudaimonia*? In what does flourishing consist? What is it to be a successful human being? Aristotle is not asking what makes us happy, and he is not concerned with the question of how we ought to lead our lives, if that question is construed as a moral one. He wants to instruct us in how to make a success of our lives.

His answer depends upon a philosophical analysis of the nature of *eudaimonia*. *Eudaimonia*, he argues, is 'an activity of the soul in accordance with excellence'. To say that *eudaimonia* is an 'activity' is to say that to flourish involves doing things as opposed to being in a certain state. (Being happy – like, say, being in love – is a state of mind: flourishing is not a state but an activity or set of activities.) To say that *eudaimonia* concerns the soul or the animator is to say that human flourishing requires the exercise of certain of the faculties by which life is defined; in particular, a person cannot be said to flourish as a human being unless he is exercising distinctively human faculties. Finally, *eudaimonia* is an activity 'in accordance with excellence'. To flourish is to do certain things excellently or well. A man who exercises his faculties but does so inefficiently or badly cannot be said to be making a success of his life.

Then what are the excellences in accordance with which we must act if we are to make a success of things? Aristotle distinguishes between excellences of character and excellences of intellect. The former include both what we think of as moral virtues – courage, generosity, fair-mindedness, and so on – and also such dispositions as a proper self-respect, an appropriate degree of ostentation, and wit; the latter include such things as knowledge, good judgement, 'practical wisdom'. In addition, Aristotle spends some time in discussing the quasi-excellence of friendship.

Men are marked off from other animals by possessing reason and the power of thought. Men 'contain something divine – what we call the intellect is divine', and our intellect is 'the divine within us'. Indeed, 'each of us actually is intellect, since this is our sovereign and best element'. The excellences most properly human, then, are the intellectual excellences, and *eudaimonia* consists primarily in activity in accordance with those excellences – it is a form of intellectual activity. 'Thus any choice or possession of the natural goods – goods of the body, wealth, friends, or any other good – which will best produce contemplation by the god [that is to say, by our intellect, the god within us], is best and is the finest standard; and any which, either because of deficiency or because of excess, prevents us from cultivating the god and from contemplating, is bad.' To flourish, to make a success of life, requires engagement in intellectual pursuits. Aristotle thought that such pursuits were immensely enjoyable, and that the intellectual life offered an unparalleled happiness; but his main thesis in the *Ethics* is not that happiness consists in intellectual activity, but that excellent intellectual activity constitutes success or flourishing for men. The intellectual giants of history may not all have been happy men, but they were all successful men: they all flourished and achieved *eudaimonia*.

20. 'Men are not isolated individuals, and the human excellences cannot be practised by hermits.' The *Nicomachean Ethics* spends much time on friendship and its varieties – which are seen here in a medieval illustration.

Intellectual activity is not enough. Men are not isolated individuals, and the human excellences cannot be practised by hermits. 'Men', Aristotle says, 'are by nature political animals'. This remark is no casual aphorism, but a piece of biological theory. 'Political animals are those which have some single activity common to them all (which is not true of all gregarious animals); such are men, bees, wasps, ants, cranes.' 'What is peculiar to men, compared to the other animals, is that they alone can perceive the good and the bad, the just and the unjust, and the rest – and it is partnership in these things which makes a household and a State.' Society and the State are not artificial trappings imposed upon natural man: they are manifestations of human nature itself.

Societies appear in different forms. The first thing to be stressed in connection with Aristotle's idea of a State is its size. 'A State cannot be made from ten men – and from 100,000 it is no longer a State.' The Greek city-states whose histories formed the factual background to Aristotle's political theory were, most of them, of pygmy proportions. They were frequently torn by faction, and their independence was ultimately destroyed by the advance of Macedonian power. Aristotle was familiar with the evils of faction (Book V of the *Politics* is given over to an analysis of the causes of civil strife), and he was intimate with the Macedonian court; yet he never lost his conviction that the small city-state was the right – the natural – form of civil society.

A State is a collection of citizens, and a citizen, in Aristotle's view, 'is defined by nothing else so well as by participation in judicial functions and in political office'. The affairs of a State are run directly by its citizens. Each citizen will be a member of the assembly or deliberative body of the nation, he will be eligible for the various offices of State, which include financial and military appointments, and he will be a part of the judiciary (for under Greek legal procedure the functions of judge and jury were not distinguished).

How much political power a citizen possessed would depend on the type of constitution which his State enjoyed, different constitutions entrusting to different persons or institutions the authority to pass legislation and to determine public policy. Aristotle produced a complex taxonomy of constitutions, the three main types of which are monarchy, aristocracy, and democracy. In certain circumstances he favoured monarchy: 'When either a whole family or an individual is so remarkable in point of excellence that his excellence exceeds that of everyone else, then it is just that that family or that individual should be king and sovereign over all matters.' But such circumstances are rare or non-existent, and in practice Aristotle preferred democracy: 'The view that the multitude, rather than a few good men, should be sovereign . . . would seem perhaps to be true. For although not each member of the multitude is a good man, still it is possible that, when they come together, they should be better – not as individuals but collectively, just as communal dinners are better than those supplied at one man's expense.'

Aristotle

A State, however constituted, must be self-sufficient, and it must achieve the goal or end for which States exist.

> It is evident that a State is not a sharing of locality for the purpose of preventing mutual harm and promoting trade. These things must necessarily be present if a State is to exist; but even if they are all present a State does not thereby exist. Rather, a State is a sharing by households and families in a good life, for the purpose of a complete and self-sufficient life.

The 'good life', which is the goal of the State, is identified with *eudaimonia*, which is the goal of individuals. States are natural entities, and like other natural objects they have a goal or end. Teleology is a feature of Aristotle's political theory no less than of his biology.

This notion of the goal of the State is linked to another high ideal. 'A fundamental principle of democratic constitutions is liberty. One form of liberty is to rule and be ruled turn and turn about. Another form is to live as one wishes; for men say that this is the aim of liberty, since to live not as one wishes is the mark of a slave.' Liberty at home is complemented by a pacific external policy; for Aristotelian States, although armed for defence, will have no imperialist ambitions. But these generous sentiments are forgotten or suppressed when Aristotle turns from generalities to particular political arrangements.

Of foreign policy he has very little to say. (But let it be noted that he is said to have urged Alexander the Great to 'deal with Greeks in the manner of a leader, with foreigners in that of a master, caring for the former as friends and relatives, treating the latter as animals or plants'.) On domestic policy he is more voluble. And it is at once evident that in fact liberty will be severely restricted in an Aristotelian State. First, liberty is the prerogative of citizens, and a large majority of the population will not possess citizenship. Women are not citizens. And there are slaves. Some men, according to Aristotle, are slaves by nature, and it is therefore permissible to make them slaves in fact. 'Someone who, being a man, belongs by nature not to himself but to someone else, is a slave by nature. He belongs to someone else if, being a man, he is an article of property – and an article of property is an instrument which aids the actions of and is separable from its owner.' Slaves may enjoy a good life – they may have kind masters. But they have no liberty and no rights.

The citizens own slaves, and they own other forms of property. Aristotle argues at length against communism. But his notion of property is a restricted one: 'Evidently it is better that property should be private – but men should make it common in use.' And he immediately adds that 'it is the task of the legislator to see that the citizens behave like this'. The State will not own the means of production, nor will it direct the economy; but the legislature will ensure that the citizens' economic behaviour is properly governed.

The voice of the State, muted in economic affairs, is strident in social matters. In the last books of the *Politics* Aristotle begins to describe his Utopia or ideal State. (The *Politics* was perhaps never completed by Aristotle: in any event, the description of Utopia is a mere fragment.) The State intervenes before birth: 'since the legislator must from the start consider how the children who are reared are to have the best physique, he must first pay attention to sexual union, determining when and between what sort of people marital relations may exist'. Intervention continues during pregnancy, and it increases during childhood, especially in connection with education:

> No one would dispute that the legislator must busy himself especially about the education of the young . . . Since the whole city has one goal, it is evident that there must also be one and the same education for everyone, and that the superintendence of this should be public and not private . . . Public matters should be publicly managed; and we should not think that each of the citizens belongs to himself, but that they all belong to the State.

Aristotle describes in considerable detail the various ways in which the State should regulate the lives of its citizens. Each regulation, however benevolent in purpose, is a curtailment of liberty; and in Aristotle's claim that the citizens 'all belong to the State' the reader will detect the infant voice of totalitarianism. If Aristotle loved liberty, he did not love it enough. His State is highly authoritarian. What has gone wrong? Some may suspect that Aristotle erred at the very first step. He confidently assigns a positive function to the State, supposing that its goal is the promotion of the good life. Given that, it is easy to imagine that the State, eager to ameliorate the human condition, may properly intervene in any aspect of human life and may compel its subjects to do whatever will make them happy. Those who see the State as a promoter of Good end up as advocates of repression. Lovers of liberty prefer to assign a negative function to the State and to regard it as a defence and protection against Evil.

Chapter 19
The Arts

Aristotle has been accused of having a narrowly intellectual view of the good life: Homer and Phidias, Rembrandt and Bach, will not, it seems, be reckoned examples of success or illustrations of *eudaimonia*. The accusation is in all probability unjust; for the ideal of 'contemplation' advanced in the *Ethics* is a large one – large enough, perhaps, to encompass a life of artistic or literary genius. However that may be, Aristotle did in practice have a considerable admiration for such genius: the admiration is apparent on every page of his surviving treatise on the arts.

The *Poetics* is short, and only one half of it still exists. It includes an essay on language and linguistics, which may be supplemented by the treatment of style in Book III of the *Rhetoric*. It says a little about the emotions, on which Aristotle writes at length and with subtlety in Book II of the *Rhetoric*. But it consists largely of what commentators have seen as literary theory or literary criticism – and in particular, of the theory and criticism of tragic drama. But that is not quite how Aristotle saw the work; for the *Poetics* is a contribution to 'productive' science; that is to say, its chief aim is to tell us not how to judge a work of art but how to produce one.

All art, Aristotle thinks, is a matter of representation or 'imitation'. 'Epic, and tragic poetry, and also comedy and dithyramb and most

21. A theatrical scene showing a master and servant setting out on a journey, depicted on a Greek vase.

flute- and harp-music, are all by and large imitations.' Art imitates or represents human life, and in particular human action. Human actions differ in character, 'and it is this difference which distinguishes tragedy from comedy; for the latter is supposed to imitate men who are worse, and the former men who are better, than those of today'. Much of the *Poetics* is devoted to tragedy. The discussion starts from a definition. 'Tragedy is an imitation of an action which is serious and complete, and which has a certain magnitude. Its language is well seasoned, with each of the kinds of seasoning used separately in its different parts. It is in dramatic, not narrative, form. And through pity and fear it accomplishes a purgation of emotions of that sort'.

Of the six elements of tragedy which Aristotle later distinguishes – plot, character, language, thought, spectacle, song – the plot is the most important: it is in virtue of its plot that a tragedy will be 'complete' or unitary, and it is through its plot that a tragedy will perform its purgative function. In particular, 'the chief means by which a tragedy works on the emotions are certain parts of the plot, namely discoveries and reversals'. The plot revolves about a central figure, the 'tragic hero' as he was later called, who must be a man 'neither pre-eminent in excellence and goodness nor falling into misfortune through badness and villainy, but rather through some mistake – a man of high reputation and good fortune, like Oedipus or Thyestes or famous men from such families'. The protagonist of a tragedy enjoys great success (Oedipus was King of Thebes) He has made some 'mistake' (Oedipus unwittingly killed his father and married his mother). The mistake is discovered, and a 'reversal' occurs (Oedipus' mother commits suicide, he blinds himself and is banished from Thebes). By its organic unity, and its implicit universality, the story works upon the feelings of the audience.

Aristotle's conception of tragedy, which had a profound effect upon the later history of European drama, is blinkered. His definition hardly fits the tragedies of Shakespeare, not to mention the works of modern playwrights whose heroes, or antiheroes, possess neither the social standing nor the grand history of an Oedipus. But Aristotle was not attempting to produce a theory of tragedy which would hold good for all time. He was telling his contemporaries, who worked within the conventions of the Greek stage, how to write a play. (His advice was based upon a mass of empirical research into the history of Greek drama.) Again, Aristotle's notion of the goal of tragedy is odd: do tragedies always, or even as a rule, purge their audience of pity and fear? And if they do so, is it plausible to regard such emotional purgation as the primary function of tragedy? (Come to that, why suppose that tragedy has a function at all?) In any event, if tragedy has an emotional aspect, it also has aesthetic and intellectual aspects.

Aristotle was aware of such aspects, even if they do not feature prominently in his definition of tragedy. Indeed, much of the *Poetics* deals implicitly with aesthetic matters, inasmuch as it discusses the 'well seasoned language' and the rhythms which tragedy requires. Of the intellectual aspect of art Aristotle has this to say:

> Everyone enjoys imitation. A sign of that is what happens in actual cases; for we enjoy looking at very accurate likenesses of things which in themselves are painful to see – for example, the forms of the foulest animals, and corpses. The reason for this is that learning is most pleasant not only to philosophers but also to other men, even if they share the pleasure only briefly. That is why we enjoy seeing likenesses – as we look, we learn and infer what each thing is, saying 'That's him.'

The pleasure of learning is an important ingredient in the productive sciences. Contemplation or the actuality of knowing is the prime component of *eudaimonia*, which is the goal of the practical sciences. Truth and knowledge are the direct aim of the theoretical sciences. The desire for knowledge, which Aristotle thought to be part of every man's nature and which was the dominant aspect of his own personality, informs and unifies the tripartite structure of Aristotelian philosophy.

Chapter 20
Afterlife

On Aristotle's death, his friend and pupil Theophrastus assumed his mantle, and under him the Lyceum remained a focus of scientific and philosophical study. But in the third century BC the light of Aristotelianism dimmed. Other schools of thought – the Stoics, the Epicureans, the Sceptics – dominated the philosophical stage, and the sciences developed separately from philosophy and became the domain of specialists.

Yet Aristotle was never forgotten, and his work enjoyed more than one renaissance. From the first to the sixth century AD, a sequence of scholarly commentators preserved his writings and revivified his thought. There was a second renewal of interest in Byzantium in the eighth century. Later, in the twelfth century, Aristotle came to Western Europe, where his texts were read by learned men and translated into Latin, and copies were widely disseminated and widely read. Aristotle was known, magisterially, as 'the Philosopher'. His thought was all-pervasive, and the half-hearted attempts by the Church to suppress his writings only confirmed their authority. For some four centuries Aristotle's philosophy and Aristotle's science ruled the West with virtually unchallenged sway.

An account of Aristotle's intellectual afterlife would be little less than a history of European thought. In part his influence was simple and direct: Aristotle's various doctrines and beliefs were purveyed as received truths, and his ideas, or their reflections, can be seen in the pages of philosophers and scientists, of historians and theologians, of poets and playwrights. But the influence also took a subtler form. The structure as well as the content of Aristotle's thought impressed itself upon posterity. The concepts and the terminology of the Lyceum provided the medium within which philosophy and science developed, so that even those radical thinkers who determined to reject Aristotelian views found themselves doing so in Aristotelian language. When today we talk of matter and form, of species and genera, of energy and potentiality, of substance and quality, of accident and essence, we unwittingly speak the language of Aristotle and think in terms and concepts which were forged in Greece two millennia ago.

It is worth adding that our modern notion of scientific method is thoroughly Aristotelian. Scientific empiricism – the idea that abstract argument must be subordinate to factual evidence, that theory is to be judged before the strict tribunal of observation – now seems a commonplace; but it was not always so, and it is largely due to Aristotle that we understand science to be an empirical pursuit. The point needs emphasizing, if only because Aristotle's most celebrated English critics, Francis Bacon and John Locke, were both staunch empiricists who thought that they were thereby breaking with the Aristotelian tradition. Aristotle was charged with preferring flimsy theories and sterile syllogisms to the solid, fertile facts. But the charge is outrageous; and it was brought by men who did not read Aristotle's own works with sufficient attention and who criticized him for the faults of his successors.

Aristotle was vastly influential. But influence and greatness are not the same thing, and we might yet ask what makes Aristotle a Master – 'the master of those who know', as Dante called him – and why he is still worth reading. His greatest single achievement was surely his biology. By the work recorded in the *Researches*, the *Parts of Animals*, and the

22. The gymnasium at Aï Khanoum in Afghanistan. The town was founded by soldiers of Alexander the Great and was visited by Aristotle's pupil Clearchus: the metaphysical fragment shown in the illustration on page 103 was discovered near the gymnasium.

Generation of Animals, he founded the science of biology, set it on a sure empirical and philosophical basis, and gave it the shape it would retain until the nineteenth century. Second only to his biology is his logic. Here too Aristotle founded a new science, and Aristotle's logic remained until the end of the last century the logic of European thought. Few men have founded one science; Aristotle apart, none has founded two.

But in biology and in logic Aristotle is outdated. If we want to learn biology or logic, we no longer turn to Aristotle's treatises: they are now of historical interest only. The same is not true of Aristotle's more philosophical writings. The essays in the *Physics*, the *Metaphysics*, and the *Ethics* are less sure, less perfect, less scientific than the logic and the biology; but they are, paradoxically, more alive. For here Aristotle has not yet been overtaken. The *Ethics*, for example, can of course be read as an historical document – as evidence for the state of practical philosophy in the fourth century BC. But it can also be read as a contribution to a contemporary debate – or rather, to an eternal debate. Contemporary philosophers read Aristotle in this fashion, treating him as a brilliant colleague.

Finally, Aristotle set before us, explicitly in his writings and implicitly in his life, an ideal of human excellence. Aristotelian man may not be the sole paragon or the unique ideal, but he is surely an admirable specimen, emulation of whom is no low ambition. I end with a passage from the *Parts of Animals* which expresses some of the best in Aristotelian man.

> Of natural substances, some we hold to be forever free from generation and destruction, others to partake in generation and destruction. The former are worthy and divine, but our studies of them are less adequate; for there is remarkably little evidence available to perception from which we might make enquiries about them and about the things we long to know. But about perishable substances – plants and

23. Aristotle and Herpyllis, according to a common medieval fantasy.

animals – we are much better off with regard to knowledge, because we are brought up among them; for anyone who is willing to take enough trouble may learn much of the truth about each kind. Each of the two sorts of substance gives pleasure: even if our grasp of the former is slight, nevertheless their value makes knowledge of them more pleasant than knowing everything here about us (just as it is more pleasant to see any small part of the things we love than to see accurately many other large things); and on the other hand, since we have better and greater knowledge of the latter sort of substances, our grasp of them has a certain superiority – and again, because they are nearer to us and more akin to our nature, they gain somewhat compared to philosophical study of things divine.

Since we have treated the latter and set down our views, we must now speak of animal nature, as far as is possible omitting nothing whether of less or greater value. For even in the case of those that are not pleasing to the senses, the nature which fashioned them nevertheless gives immeasurable pleasures to the student who can discern the causes of things and is naturally of a philosophical turn. For it would be irrational and absurd if, while we take pleasure in contemplating the likenesses of such natural things inasmuch as we contemplate at the same time the skill of the painter or the sculptor who fashioned them, we should yet fail to find more pleasure in the contemplation of the natural things themselves, particularly if we can discern their causes. Thus we should not childishly complain against the enquiry into the less worthy animals; for in everything natural there is something marvellous.

Heraclitus is reported to have said to some visitors who wished to meet him and who hesitated when they saw him warming himself at the stove: 'Come in, be bold: there are gods here too.' In the same way we should approach the study of every animal without shame; for in all of them there is something natural and something beautiful.

References

All works cited are by Aristotle unless otherwise stated. References to Aristotle's writings normally consist of an abbreviated title, a book number (in Roman numerals), a chapter number (Arabic), and a specification of page, column, and line in the standard edition of the Greek text by Immanuel Bekker. (Most subsequent editions of the Greek and most English translations print Bekker references in their margins at regular intervals.) There is no universally agreed set of abbreviations. The set I have adopted is fairly standard. Where there is a mismatch between the abbreviated and the full version of the title, that is because the abbreviations are based on the Latin translation of the Greek titles. So, for example, *Meteor* II 9, 369a31, refers to line 31 of column a on page 369 of Bekker's edition, a line which occurs in the ninth chapter of the second book of Aristotle's *Meteorology*.

Abbreviations

An	*On the Soul*
APr	*Prior Analytics*
APst	*Posterior Analytics*
Cael	*On the Heavens*
Cat	*Categories*
EE	*Eudemian Ethics*
EN	*Nicomachean Ethics*
GA	*Generation of Animals*

GC	*On Generation and Corruption*
HA	*History of Animals*
Int	*On Interpretation*
MA	*Movement of Animals*
Met	*Metaphysics*
Meteor	*Meteorology*
PA	*Parts of Animals*
Phys	*Physics*
Poet	*Poetics*
Pol	*Politics*
Protr	*Protrepticus*
Rhet	*Rhetoric*
Soph El	*Sophistical Refutations*
Top	*Topics*

Page

3   (1) all men: *Met* I 1, 980a22

    (2) the activity: *Met* XII 7, 1072b27

    (3) the acquisition: *Protr* fragment 52 Rose = B 56 Düring, quoted by Iamblichus, *Protrepticus* 40.20–41.2

    (4) we must not: *EN* X 7, 1177b31–5

4   he wrote: Diogenes Laertius, *Lives of the Philosophers* V 21

5   In every form: *Rhet* III 1, 1404a8–12

6   he surrounds: Atticus, fragment 7 (p. 28 ed. Baudry), quoted by Eusebius, *Preparation for the Gospel* XV ix 14, 810D

9   he did not want: Aelian, *Varia historia* III 36

11 (1) an inscription: Ibn Abi Usaibia, *Life of Aristotle* 18, printed in I. Düring, *Aristotle in the Ancient Biographical Tradition* (Göteborg, 1957), p. 215

    (2) they drew up: W. Dittenberger (ed.), *Sylloge inscriptionum Graecarum* (3rd ed., Leipzig, 1915), no. 275

    (3) as for what: *Letters*, fragment 9 [in M. Plezia (ed.), *Aristoteles: Privatorum scriptorum fragmenta* (Leipzig, 1977)], quoted by Aelian, *Varia historia* XIV 1

14   the city of Assos: T. Dorandi (ed.), *Filodemo: Storia dei filosofi* (Naples, 1991), col V (p. 129)

18   First, let us: *HA* I 6, 491a19–21

19   The octopus: *HA* IV 1, 524a3–20

20   (1) this is plain: *HA* V 8, 542a2–6
       (2) it defends itself: *HA* IX 45, 630b8–11

21   (1) are generated: *HA* V 19, 551a1–7
       (2) *an experiment*: *HA* VI 3, 561a6–562a20

22   the so-called *teuthoi*: *HA* IV 1, 524a25–8

24   (1) inflamed: Pliny, *Natural History* VIII xvi 44
       (2) Their error: *GA* III 5, 756a31–4

25   (1) he worked: anon., *Vita Aristotelis Marciana* 6 (in Düring, op. cit., p. 98)
       (2) he is the first: Strabo, *Geography* XIII i 54
       (3) one should make: *Top* I 14, 105b12–15
       (4) we have given: *Met* I 3, 983a33–b6

26   in the case: *Soph El* 34, 184a9–b9

28   (1) for if the difficulties: *EN* VII 1, 1145b6–7
       (2) In all cases: *Soph El* 34, 183b18–27

29   Investigation. *Met* II 1, 993a30–b5, b11–19

30   why did he: Philodemus, *On Rhetoric* col. LIII 41–2 (vol. II, pp. 57–8 Sudhaus)

31   at once gave up: *Nerinthus*, fragment 64 Rose, quoted by Themistius, *Oration* XXXIII 295D

33   In the gymnasium: Epicrates, fragment 11 Kock, quoted by Athenaeus, *Deipnosophists* 59D

35   (1) whom it is not right: *Poems*, fragment 3 (in Plezia, op. cit.), quoted by Olympiodorus, *Commentary on the Gorgias* 41.9
       (2) Plato used: Aelian, *Varia historia* IV 9

40   (1) The causes: *Met* XII 4, 1070a31–3
       (2) all thought: *Met* VI 1, 1025b25
       (3) there are three: *Met* VI 1, 1026a18–19

41   (1) If there are: *Met* VI 1, 1026a26–30
       (2) the theoretical: *Met* VI 1, 1026a22–3

75 (1) nature is: *Phys* III 1, 200b12
 (2) things have a nature: *Phys* II 1, 192b32

77 (1) there is something: *Phys* V 1, 224a34–b3
 (2) there is no change: *Phys* III 1, 200b323; VI 4, 234b29

78 (1) whatever comes: *Met* VII 8, 1033b12–13
 (2) it becomes clear: *Phys* I 7, 190b1–8

79 Change is: *Phys* III 1, 201a10–11

80 (1) actuality is: *Met* IX 8, 1049b10–12
 (2) in all cases: *Met* IX 8, 1049b24–7

83 A thing is called: *Phys* II 3, 194b23–195a3

84 the because-of-which: *Met* VII 17, 1041a23–7

86 (1) the cause is: *APst* II 2 90a7

54 (2) what it is: *APst* II 2, 90a15–18

87 Why did: *APst* II 11, 94a36–b2

88 Why is there: *APst* II 11, 94b9

89 (1) Since things: *Phys* II 3, 195a4–8
 (2) both because: *APst* II 11, 94b32–4

91 And that there is: *Met* VI 2, 1027a20–2

92 and for that: *An* III 8, 432a7–9

43 All animals: *APst* II 19, 99b35–100a9

94 the cause: *GA* III 5, 756a2–b

96 (1) *reliability of the senses*: *An* III 3, 428b18–25
 (2) It is evident: *Met* IV 4, 1008b12–16
 (3) they are really: *Met* IV 5, 1010b4–9

97 a scribe: Suda, s.v. Aristoteles

98 I have already: *Meteor* I 1, 338a20–7; 339a7–9

100 Of the parts: *HA* I 1, 486a5–8; 13–14

101 (1) Circular motion: *GC* II 11, 338a18–b6
 (2) Our remote: *Met* XII 8, 1074b1–10
 (3) god seems: *Met* I 2, 983a8–9

102 (1) there is some other: *Cael* I 2, 269b14–16
 (2) it is the function: *PA* IV 10, 686a29
 (3) we tend: *Cael* II 12, 292a19–22, b1–2
 (4) must there be: *MA* 4, 699b31–5

Chronological Table

Further Reading

All Aristotle's surviving works are to be found in English translation in the 'Oxford Translation':

- J. Barnes (ed.), *The Complete Works of Aristotle* (Princeton NJ, 1984).

The volumes in the Loeb Classical Library contain English versions with Greek on facing pages. Many of Aristotle's works are available in Oxford Classics, in Penguin, and in other paperback series. The Clarendon Aristotle series supplies close translations and philosophical commentaries on several of Aristotle's major writings.

The classic edition of the Greek text, by Immanuel Bekker, was published in Berlin in 1831. Modern editions may be found in such collections as the Oxford Classical Texts, the Loeb Classical Library, the Teubner Library, and the Budé series.

Of the countless general books on Aristotle's thought, I may mention:

- J. L. Ackrill, *Aristotle the Philosopher* (Oxford, 1981).
- G. Grote, *Aristotle* (London, 1883).
- G. E. R. Lloyd, *Aristotle* (Cambridge, 1968).
- W. D. Ross, *Aristotle* (London, 1923).

The essays in:
- J. Barnes (ed.), *The Cambridge Companion to Aristotle* (Cambridge, 1995)

collectively provide a comprehensive introduction to Aristotelian philosophy; and the volume has a large bibliography to guide more advanced study.

The evidence for Aristotle's life [Ch 1–2] is assembled and discussed in:
- I. Düring, *Aristotle in the Ancient Biographical Tradition* (Göteborg, 1957)

and there is an account of the Lyceum in:
- J. P. Lynch, *Aristotle's School* (Berkeley, CA, 1972).

On his zoology and biology [Ch 3–4] two older works are worth reading:
- G. H. Lewes, *Aristotle – A Chapter from the History of Science* (London, 1864).
- W. d'A. Thompson, *On Aristotle as a Biologist* (London, 1912).

On the philosophical – that is to say, the Platonic – background to Aristotle's work [Ch 5] see:
- G. E. L. Owen, 'The Platonism of Aristotle', in his *Logic, Science and Dialectic* (London, 1986).

The idea of an axiomatized deductive science [Ch 6] is analysed in:
- H. Scholz, 'The ancient axiomatic theory', in J. Barnes, M. Schofield and R. Sorabji (eds), *Articles on Aristotle* I (London, 1975).

On logic and on knowledge [Ch 7–8] see:
- G. Patzig, *Aristotle's Theory of the Syllogism* (Dordrecht, 1968).
- C. C. W. Taylor, 'Aristotle's epistemology', in S. Everson (ed.),

Companions to Ancient Thought: 1 – Epistemology (Cambridge, 1990).

There is a classic paper on the 'aporetic' aspect of Aristotle's thought [Ch 9]:
- G. E. L. Owen, '*Tithenai ta phainomena*', in his *Logic, Science and Dialectic* (London, 1986).

Many of the issues raised by Aristotle's metaphysical speculations [Ch 6, 10] are aired in Parts I and II of:
- T. H. Irwin, *Aristotle's First Principles* (Oxford, 1988).

Note also, on the 'categories' and on ambiguity:
- M. Frede, 'Categories in Aristotle', in his *Essays on Ancient Philosophy* (Oxford, 1987).
- G. E. L. Owen, 'Logic and metaphysics in some earlier works of Aristotle', in his *Logic, Science and Dialectic* (London, 1986).
- G. E. L. Owen, 'Aristotle on the snares of ontology', in his *Logic, Science and Dialectic* (London, 1986).

Further Reading

On change and causation and also on teleology [Ch 11-12, 17] see:
- R. Sorabji, *Necessity, Cause and Blame* (London, 1980).

On Aristotle's empiricism and on the relation between theory and evidence [Ch 13, 16]:
- G. E. R. Lloyd, 'Empirical research in Aristotle's biology', in his *Methods and Problems in Greek Science* (Cambridge, 1991).
- P. Pellegrin, *Aristotle's Classification of Animals* (Berkeley CA, 1986).

For a general description of Aristotle's natural world [Ch 14] see:
- F. Solmsen, *Aristotle's System of the Physical World* (Ithaca NY, 1960).

For his psychological views [Ch 15] see:
- S. Everson, *Aristotle on Perception* (Oxford, 1997).

On practical philosophy [Ch 18], there are two short books on ethics:
- D. S. Hutchinson, *The Virtues of Aristotle* (London, 1986)
- J. O. Urmson, *Aristotle's Ethics* (Oxford, 1987)

and a long book on politics:
- F. D. Miller, *Nature, Justice, and Rights in Aristotle's Politics* (Oxford, 1995).

For art and poetry [Ch 19] see the papers collected in:
- A. O. Rorty (ed.), *Essays on Aristotle's* Poetics (Princeton NJ, 1992).

On Aristotle's afterlife [Ch 20] see:
- R. Sorabji (ed), *Aristotle Transformed* (London, 1990).

Index

Aristotle

Index

Aristotle

Expand your collection of
VERY SHORT INTRODUCTIONS

Visit the
VERY SHORT INTRODUCTIONS
Web site

www.oup.co.uk/vsi

➤ **Information** about all published titles

➤ News of **forthcoming books**

➤ **Extracts** from the books, including titles not yet published

➤ **Reviews** and views

➤ **Links** to other **web sites** and main OUP web page

➤ Information about **VSIs in translation**

➤ **Contact** the editors

➤ **Order** other **VSIs** on-line

LOGIC
A Very Short Introduction
Graham Priest

Logic is often perceived as an esoteric subject, having little to do with the rest of philosophy, and even less to do with real life. In this lively and accessible introduction, Graham Priest shows how wrong this conception is. He explores the philosophical roots of the subject, explaining how modern formal logic deals with issues ranging from the existence of God and the reality of time to paradoxes of self-reference, change and probability. Along the way, the book explains the basic ideas of formal logic in simple, non-technical, terms, as well as the philosophical pressures to which these have responded. This is a book for anyone who has ever been puzzled by a piece of reasoning.

'This book is terrific. ... It covers a lot of ground, but in a wonderfully relaxed and interesting way.'

Simon Blackburn, University of North Carolina

'This is a delightful and engaging introduction to the basic concepts of logic. Whilst not shirking the problems, Priest always manages to keep his discussion accessible and instructive.'

Adrian Moore, St Hugh's College, Oxford

www.oup.co.uk/vsi/logic

ANCIENT PHILOSOPHY

A Very Short Introduction

Julia Annas

The tradition of ancient philosophy is a long, rich and varied one, in which a constant note is that of discussion and argument. This book aims to introduce readers to some ancient debates and to get them to engage with the ancient developments of philosophical themes. Getting away from the presentation of ancient philosophy as a succession of Great Thinkers, the book aims to give readers a sense of the freshness and liveliness of ancient philosophy, and of its wide variety of themes and styles.

'Incisive, elegant, and full of the excitement of doing philosophy, Julia Annas's Short Introduction boldly steps outside of conventional chronological ways of organizing material about the Greeks and Romans to get right to the heart of the human problems that exercised them, problems ranging from the relation between reason and emotion to the objectivity of truth. I can't think of a better way to begin.'

Martha Nussbaum, University of Chicago

www.oup.co.uk/vsi/ancientphilosophy